1909	1910	1912	1918	1921	1921	1922	1923	1927	1928	1930	1932	1935

Thomas F. Ryan invents 5-pin bowling in Toronto, Ontario. Original pin count is established as "4-2-1-3-5"

First league formed

Rubber band added to pin

First 400 game bowled by Alfred Shrubb

First 450 perfect game bowled by Bill Bromfield

First ladies 5-pin bowling league started by Marion Dibble in Toronto

first inter-city match between Toronto and Montreal using a telephone hookup

Winnipeg's Charles Gibson introduces 5-pin bowling to Western Canada

First bowling organization: Canadian Bowling Association

First official rule book printed

Western Canada adopts own scoring system. Pin values equal "1-4-5-3-2"

First sanctioned 450 by Joe Heenan

Blind bowlers' leagues introduced in Western Canada

BOWLBRAWL © 2005 Nathaniel G. Moore
Edited by Andy Brown
First Edition

Excerpts have been published, often in a different format, in the following publications:
Forget, Matrix, Half Empty, Grimm

Library and Archives Canada Cataloguing in Publication

Moore, Nathaniel G
Bowlbrawl / Nathaniel G. Moore.
ISBN 1-894994-10-8
1. Towell, Robert. 2. Bowlers — Canada — Biography.
I. Title.
GV902.T68M66 2005   794.6'092   C2005-905886-2

Published by our friends at:
CONUNDRUM PRESS
PO Box 55003, CSP Fairmount, Montreal, Quebec, H2T 3E2, Canada
conpress@ican.net • http://home.ican.net/~conpress

Dépot Legal, Bibliothèque nationale du Québec
Printed and bound in Canada on 100% recycled, ancient rainforest friendly paper.

conundrum press acknowledges the financial assistance of the
Canada Council for the Arts toward its publishing program.

**Canada Council
for the Arts**   **Conseil des Arts
du Canada**

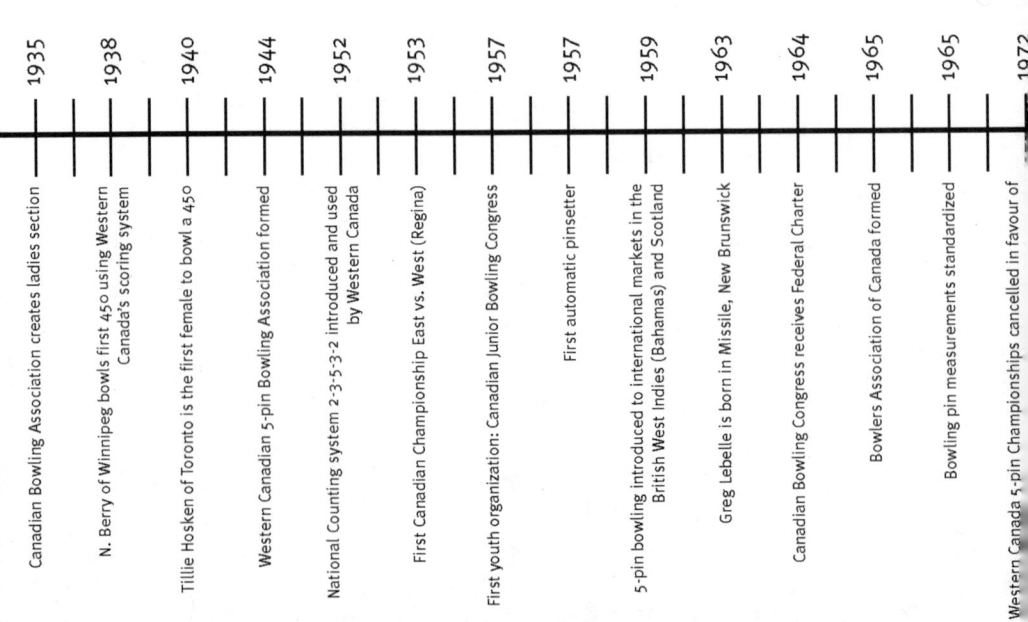

NATHANIEL G. MOORE

1972	1972	1975	1976	1978	1978	1980	1984	1987	1990	1995	1996	1999	2000

Golden Age Bowler's Club formed

Robert Towell is born just north of Toronto, Ontario

680,000 bowlers in Canada bowl 5-pins weekly in over 20,000 leagues. 102 local bowling associations with 105,000 members affiliated with the Canadian Bowling Congress

Nikola Gisella is born in Montreal, Quebec

Dragan Momchilo is born in Ajax, Ontario

Canadian Bowling Congress and Bowling Association of Canada dissolved: Canadian 5-Pin Bowler's Association formed

First international Bowling Cup competition held in Manila between Canada and the Philippines

5-pin bowling celebrates its 75th anniversary

National 5-pin Bowler's Ranking introduced by Canadian 5-pin Bowler's Association

Use of personal bowling balls allowed

521,000 Canadians participate regularly in 5-pin bowling (37% Male 63% Female)

Robert Towell launches World Championship Bowling in Toronto

World Championship Bowling announces the collapse of the league

Greg Lebelle's infamous bowling assault trial takes centre stage at Old City Hall in Toronto, Ontario

The deer on Pine Mountain,
Where there are no falling leaves,
Knows the coming of autumn
Only by the sound of his own voice

— Onakatomi No Yoshinobu

It was Sunday morning. Frowning in his unlit bedroom, young Robert Towell sat on his bed with his unlaced bowling shoes on his feet. Barely audible were the hums from lawnmower parts, doing their cyclical job while the odd Christian trotted off to church for Easter service.

Robert sat, pensive and upset. His nylon shorts and crappy yellow and brown T-shirt with a bowling logo were snug around his scrawny frame. He was three months shy of his eleventh birthday. Despite the rumours of a sequel to the videogame and pizza marathon of previous annual celebrations, the young athlete was not excited in any way. In fact, like most events in his life at the time, he found the whole experience rather pedestrian.

"Come on champ, it's game time," his father said with poor articulation from the other side of the door.

Robert Towell had tried to look on the bright side; he was doing well in a sport that demanded relatively nothing of him, and he was making money. The skill came naturally to him. No lactic acid built up in his joints, and his muscles were rarely sore. Occasionally, he'd do laps around the parking lot before and after the matches to avoid feeling stiff.

He wasn't intimidated by meeting fresh competition, sponsors, interviewers or rival coaches. Nor was he shy around the adults who pawed and positioned him like a prize-winning window ham. He even got a kick out of the constant flashbulbs, interviews and colour print ads at pro shops. But he did not feel heroic, despite the countless ribbons and trophies that gathered dust in his room.

"Come on Robbie, get your coat on," his mother joined in.

The thick tea-coloured curtains were drawn tight, but it didn't matter, it was as if the boy had never seen the sun to begin with.

Bowling was becoming a permanent theatre of mediocrity that he couldn't stomach much longer. He wanted the bigger picture. He wanted to feel more things.

Underground and removed, at least three times a week (if not more) he participated in a shameful bad lung Olympics. Away from the veins of the sun, positioned like a far off moon, young Robert Towell was paid to play, paid to stay out of the sunlight, off the surface of the green earth and sequestered, inhaling the various brands of second and third-hand smoke passed down to him by his elders.

His polyester parental units thudded redundantly on his thinning bedroom door for more. More of the same. Robert got up and walked towards the noise, then stopped. Through a slight gap in his curtains he peered outside and saw the vibrant colours of the afternoon. But he could not return the feeling of joy that accompanied this climate, and frowned at the teasing sunscape. To him, sunlight, splashes, licorice laughs were as alien as senility.

It was game time again.

He got back on the bed and held his breath in unsubtle protest, trying to stop any further respiratory activity. He had not yet learned to snicker, but knew that he was a few months shy of fully developing a vindictive gene. He was a patient kid, with hair as dark as fine silk, and as flat, and, if washed properly, as shiny.

On occasions such as these, he could feel himself outgrowing his thoughts, as if they were clothes that could never possibly be with him for eternity. Nothing, he thought, accepting his fate for the day, would remain of this. He listened to his parents mutter and warm up for another round of cawing.

"Robbie, come on!" his Dad boomed, clearing his throat. Young Robert imagined his father's coughs being carefully pointed and shot through the keyhole.

It wasn't the sport that Robert Towell despised so much as the buildings themselves. However, as he discovered over the course of his career, both came hand in hand. At night, crippled with disgust, he lay awake trying to isolate the sport from the underground prison, like a scientist tries to weed theory from serum, but it never worked.

In sleep his dreams always began in the same way, like the early stages of a stroke or a bad rash. There were elements of a hospital emergency room, that sort of chaotic necessity to keep moving down the bright hallway, a pulsing fever, then the smell, the stink of over-brewed coffee muttering and bleeding thick in the skin the bowling alley, the structure that acted as host to the disease. Here, the lousy music, the out of season food, the piercing PA system, the thick sound of scuffed carpets as if tongues not feet were traversing their foul hides, the butts in the ashtray and the trashy bingo-soaked clientele were all unavoidable side-effects. Sleep drove him into a netherworld of calm, but only for a few short hours.

"Sewer sport," Robert Towell mumbled, looking at his curtains.

There were some good elements about the game, he knew this, they were just too ensconced below the filth. It needed fresh air. In his desperate fantasies the game would be as vulnerable as a fat piñata; the sun would melt the pins, gusts of clean air would blow the balls off the ball return, the score machine would explode with an awesome and volcanic crack. But always, without fail, something would always go terribly wrong, the game would be there the next day. Young Robert prayed for a coma.

"Robert Jacob Towell, get out here this instant," his father bellowed.

With knees up and apart, he stalled for time and retied his shoes, then stared blankly through his legs at his locked door. He looked down at his dirt brown bowling shoes with the yellow swirl on the sides.

"Quit yelling, just start the car okay." His mother tried to calm Robert's father. "Robert," his mother pleaded, "Jerry's coming to watch, he's in the car, I even made you guys some banana bread for the ride."

Jerry, Robert thought. *At least he'll make it bearable, a familiar face. He'll eat all my chips. Oh well.*

With keys rattling, his father tried one last time, but on this one-way exchange, decided to use a slightly more calm and articulate delivery.

"Robert, we have to leave now son, it's an important match."

Robert felt the delivery was insincere at best, almost like a bad BBC commercial for soap or fish food. He clenched his fists and placed his pillow against his open mouth. He listened to the tone of his father's voice as it unravelled, noting its low-tech monotone sincerity only found on the reels of primary biology films about the benefits of studying ants at odd hours. *The ant is a fascinating creature, as strong as a tank, and smarter than Einstein and Hitler combined. If ants were as large as humans, we would be slaves.*

"Come on son." His father's anger couldn't be restrained, the pressure could not be repressed, and young Robert Towell felt a tightening in his stomach.

"There you are, good, now let's go," his mother said with a smile so fake it looked like it was put together with scotch tape. He grudgingly entered the car and felt, all too briefly, his skin mix with the sun, kissed goodbye for another day, unable to linger in the sweet exchange.

Soon he would be underground.

There was no comfort. There was nothing.

Robert Towell closed his eyes in the backseat as the sounds of children engulfed in the bounty of nature clogged his ears: fresh air, endless grass stains, knee-scrapes and bicycle chain malfunctions.

As they drove, Robert munched on banana bread and noticed his best friend Jerry Tomlin was also munching on banana bread. Robert envied very little about Jerry, except for his obvious and consistent tan, light brown hair, the benefits, Robert hissed to himself, of the greenhouse effect.

The family car pulled into the bowling alley, where a television camera operator and reporter were in the middle of an interview with Robert's coach, Billy Guthrie. Guthrie was a middle-aged bowling enthusiast with balding red hair and beady little brown eyes. He was semi-retired, and worked on occasion at a health supply store for pets. His wife made kites which weren't very sturdy and rarely got off the ground, but their main source of income was from the Guthries' penny-pinching lifestyle. He had started to wrinkle around the mouth, and when he spoke, the occasional rattle could be heard, either from his lungs or teeth. Guthrie waved as the family car came to a stop. Robert inhaled deeply and unbuckled his safety belt.

"Hey Robbie, there's your coach," his mother said with enthusiasm. She was rummaging through her purse for a small plastic bag of digestive cookies. Robert sighed and shook, closing his eyes tightly, and running his hands through his hair, hoping the coach wasn't referring to him on air as *Bobby* — the shortened version of his name that made him want to carve faces with broken ice skate blades endlessly.

The interviewer smiled and waited for her cue. The cue came.

"Coach Guthrie, what can the folks at home expect from your bowler this afternoon?"

"Well gosh, Bobby is doing real well, each week he's improving on so many levels. He's had to memorize lines for the show's weekly promos and has had to spend countless hours getting three strikes in a row for these spots. What else can I tell ya? There's talk of him doing some more commercial work too. He's really comfortable with it. And the tournament offers come in every week, so he's going to be a busy boy."

BILLY GUTHRIE

Swimming Team 56-57; Bowling Club 56-57; "B" Team Baseball; "A" Team Football

To get out of high school this year

"Are you nervous?" Jerry asked, licking his fingers of banana bread.

"I don't get nervous. I just do this. I go and do this. There is no emotion once I go underground."

"I'm thirsty."

"I can get you some pop. I know the chef."

"Your coach is waving to you."

"Don't look. Look at me. Or, over here. He drinks tons."

"Of beer?"

"No. Gingerale."

Deep in the poorly ventilated underground sports chamber, the camera operators began the show with a long swooping establishment shot that included several lanes and the crowd.

Coach Billy Guthrie, sipping on the first of many afternoon bottles of gingerale with two straws, approached young Robert Towell, surrounded by a crew member who was doing a light reading, as well as his mother who was orbiting around the boy. Robert was scraping the bottoms of his bowling shoes in juvenile disgust and adjusting his wrist guards as his mother parted his dark hair.

"Mom, cut it out," he said.

"I just don't want you to have bad hair on the television," she said.

"Thanks Mom, you're really helping my game. Can you just go sit in the stands and be annoying, from like, way over there."

"Oh Robert."

"Thanks."

Robert's mother joined her husband who was boring several of the other parents with unmitigated enthusiasm about the municipal garbage pick-up service. Jerry Tomlin sat sipping on cola, feet dangling on a stool at the snack bar, and watched the activity with a veneer of carefree indifference. He had chubby cheeks but was not at all fat, and had scattered bangs that usually blocked his blue eyes.

For over three years now, every weekend was spent chained to the ball return, while parents were fist-fighting in the stands. There was pressure to do the job amidst unavoidable exploitation. Robert Towell tried to dodge all the nausea yet he felt the germs forming civilizations all over the bowling trophy, sullied with a thousand fingerprints.

Coach Billy Guthrie patted young Robert Towell on the shoulder.

"Bobby, you ready?"

There was nothing endearing about the moment. Robert Towell looked at Guthrie and nodded, wanting to vomit a hot lava on the man's feet and watch him topple over. Then he'd spit on his coach's fresh stumps and walk across his bad back to the snack bar. But a part of the boy knew he could win, and that somehow, being better than everyone else at something, at least for a moment, was as good a way as any to spend an afternoon captive with a bunch of crummy adults.

The match began with his opponent registering a bland spare. The crowd hissed in apathy. Robert Towell countered with a strike, he even pointed to the camera with a cocky snort. The camera work, honest at best, captured the mood: the chattering crowd, his parents in the stands. As the camera panned across Mom and Dad, the broadcaster made note of their existence in the frame, using words like *proud* and *supportive* as the camera focused in on the soft edges of Mrs. Towell's baby blue nylon winter coat complete with the hot chocolate stain from the previous week.

"Go on Robbie, you can take him!" she barked.

At the ball return, Robert Towell paced, taking time to eye the crowd, his opponent, his coach, and the floor director who was twitching in every direction. His same-aged opponent snarled and answered with a confident strike of his own.

"Beat that Towell-head," the boy taunted with a bit of tongue. Robert responded with his own tongue extended coupled with excessive blinking, resembling someone being electrocuted.

Mrs. Towell began to cheer louder, even getting up on her own two feet and cupping the sides of her mouth. The crowd's energy, even with the addition of his mother's bellowing did nothing for Robert Towell. He could win. He didn't need the audience's passive existence to accomplish these menial physical feats.

"Bor-ing," he mumbled. He could not be beat. He knew it. He knew the routine now: win, win, win, sleep, win, out for dinner, big chocolate sundae, feel the acidic turmoil negotiate its course and forget about the game for another night. That was the routine, bland, reliable and predictable, and he felt calmed by its consistent polarity in his life.

Mrs. Towell: "He's good Robbie, watch out, remember what I told you." He remembered nothing; he felt darkness inside of his body, like a primary school piece of black felt, cut with safety scissors. He was embarrassed, his parents looked like farm hands while he looked at best like a Sears catalogue hostage.

Robert Towell could hear his father muttering in between primal bites of his crap-stand hot dog purchase, the pieces of meat slapping against his decaying molars and inner jaw.

"Robert, come on son!" Mr. Towell aped out, his neck turning in neurotic twists.

The match continued with both boys taking the lead over each other. For a brief stretch Towell and his opponent were matching one another pin for pin. Sensing a threat to his championship reign (for he was back in the Under-15 Provincial 5-pin Finals for the second year in a row) young Robert Towell put an extra bit of spin on his ball in the ninth frame, a dangerous technique that did not always pan out in practice. But this was no practice. He nailed it and answered his opponent's spare with a strike to finish the match 179-167.

Robert Towell's face was still, he said nothing to his opponent, not even stopping to look at him or shake his hand. When it was handed to him, he held aloft the Under-15 Provincial 5-pin trophy as the camera crew and host swarmed. He looked into the camera with dead grey eyes that began to well up in chameleon tears, but he sucked it up. He could smell the sun on some of the spectators. It was lust.

HE REMEMBERED NOTHING, HE FELT DARKNESS INSIDE OF HIS BODY, LIKE A PRIMARY SCHOOL PIECE OF BLACK FELT, CUT WITH SAFETY SCISSORS. HE WAS EMBARRASSED, HIS PARENTS LOOKED LIKE FARM HANDS WHILE HE LOOKED AT BEST LIKE A SEARS CATALOGUE HOSTAGE.

It wasn't over; there was more to come. Another alley, another late afternoon tournament. Robert scanned the crowd for his friend Jerry, dodging eager waves from complete strangers who were, as Towell would later reflect, "most likely pedophiles who were stalking me for some torturous mansion basement life I thankfully avoided."

Jerry Tomlin looked at his sneakers, his head lowered, trying not to envy the fanfare for his friend Robert. As adults mussed his hair, patted him too hard on his back, Robert winced and coughed. Young Robert hated the puke postmodern abstract carpet designs that melded the colours of fox orange and Aqua Velva blue, with hints of spray-paint pink long faded. This was the young boy's childhood, kept sealed in a jar, the sun never lubricating his mind or body, never warming the back of his neck. Instead, overcooked hot dogs from the darkest caverns of Ontario flipped, never vilified by the health inspector. *One day,* thought Robert Towell, *I will murder each rule, each pin, and unthread each stitch in this foul, pleated sport.*

The Man Who Murdered Bowling
BY ROBERT TOWELL

FROM CHAPTER SEVEN: HOW I BECAME A GODDAMN PUMPKIN

I remember auditioning for *Pumpkin Seeds* very well. It was the year I turned pro, in a sense, I mean, I became a man. Even at 15, I had a sense of wanting to start a family of my own, or at least I had urges that pushed me towards an uncontrollable independence. Jerry Tomlin, who lived around the corner from me, or so he said, was bit by the acting bug too, and followed me to that audition. He was a bit taller, a bit heavier, but he didn't have the sort of glint in his eyes that I did. But yeah Jerry Tomlin and I lied and told our parents we were going bowling. Of course, because of my undeniable talent, good looks and schoolboy charisma, I landed the part of Michael Pumpkin on the spot. Jerry Tomlin was not so lucky. He wasn't even cast as a classmate or paperboy extra. He was really off that day; I told him to get a haircut, and also not to wear his shiny sports jacket, the baseball one which I thought was too adolescent or something, too eager. I dressed sort of preppy, but not too preppy. Anyway, the scene was from the pilot where my teacher scolds me for talking in class, and my timing was undeniable. They loved me. For the first four months, with little effort, I told my parents I was interning at Swiss Chalet and that all the kids in the neighbourhood were interning at different chains, whether it was stationery retail, automotive therapy or baking supplies. I told them never to visit me at work, that I was very dedicated to learning a new trade and that I couldn't obtain people skills doing a paper route alone like some serial killer at 5:30 in the morning. I wasn't one of those slow kids who could earn money before anyone was even awake. I wanted middle management exposure. I told them I would also be on the road three or four nights a week. They didn't seem to mind. I arranged to have all my scripts sent to Swiss Chalet where I would go twice a week to pick up my mail and daub myself in their spicy gravy. The scripts always came in a blue folder which was inside a white envelope, which, by the time it reached me, was pawed up in gravy prints.

THE TOWELL HOME

The heat scolded his youth. In the new arena of sun, Robert Towell impregnated himself with the rarity of sunstroke. He relished the natural heat of the stagnant summer. In white shorts and a blue Ralph Lauren Polo golf shirt he had been in his driveway playing evil God with the garden hose, taking care of a few excess ant hills while blasting the neighbours hedges off his property line. "I hated them for growing their crap in my driveway; it was bad enough I had to smell their cooking, I didn't want to have to deal with their choice of horticulture as well."[1]

The year was 1987. George Michael's album *Faith* had just been released in North America and the first single, "I Want Your Sex", became young Robert Towell's professional and spiritual mantra. It was the opening song on Side A and he especially liked listening all the way to the end of the LP for "I Want Your Sex Part 3", with its proclamation that to avoid killing people on the road one should, as Towell interpreted, "stay where you are and have drunk sex all night."

He entertained thoughts of post-bowling television stardom on the set of *Pumpkin Seeds*. "I was nervous inside the yellowing world of professional bowling, it really creeped me out. I thought the sport was going nowhere, and felt that I had lost a lot of ground on the idea of childhood, and since my family was in a constant state of consumer vanity I needed the comfort of a real childhood, even if it was entirely scripted. Even if the sunshine was scripted at least there was the intent of sunshine. Bowling didn't bring me closer to my family, they seemed to lose interest in me. When they did express interest it was only to scold me for wanting to quit. Honestly, I knew that I had done everything I could have hoped to accomplish in the sport. It may sound vain, but I am vain."

At the age of fifteen, Robert Towell had finished his bowling career with an impressive six year run (1981-1987) with accolades that included seven provincial championships, seven major provincial sponsorships, one national sponsorship, sixteen house league records, nine league records (under 10), nineteen tournament records (under 15), as well as being named bowler-of-the-week on CHCH's *Teen Bowling Ontario* a record 76 times.

---

[1] From an early draft of *The Man Who Murdered Bowling*.

Robert was cast as Michael Pumpkin out of 193 applicants. Nikola Gisella made the cut to play his sister after seven grueling callbacks, and a bevy of high-strung Carol Pumpkin wannabees. "I remember the auditions," she said, "the room smelled like watermelon bubblegum."

When Robert met Nikola on set, he shivered awkwardly. "I was standing next to the air conditioner and had a few glasses of ice water on the go." Nonetheless, it was a moment he would never forget. "There was something special about the tiny set and the little sandwiches left out for the cast and crew each day at 3:15 PM. Nikola and I had the same tutor, the same driver, the same script assistant, and the same make-up artist."

To insure the siblings would meld, the director had them also share their lunch breaks, have the same gym time, same toy store runaround time and virtually identical public appearance schedules.

"All right, quiet on the set," the floor director yelled. Robert Towell was wearing a striped turtleneck, grey, orange and blue. The kitchen was done up suppertime style. A curly blond mother in a pastel blouse and tight grey slacks put a bowl of mashed potatoes on the kitchen table as the father, Jason Pumpkin, in a dark knit sweater, tan pants and a well-ironed collar added the salad and two bottles of

Maggie Pumpkin:
Michael! Dinner.

Jason Pumpkin:
How was your day Carol?

Carol Pumpkin:
Fine Dad.

Maggie:
Michael! Dinner!

Michael enters.

Maggie:
Michael when I call you, answer me.

Michael:
I was watching a bird build a nest.

Jason:
And Michael, how was *your* first day back at school?

Michael:
I think the desks missed having me around all summer.

Laugh Track

Jason:
Seriously, how is your teacher?

Maggie:
Oh isn't it Ms. Jennings? I hear she's really nice.

Michael:
My teacher is nice. She smells like apples.

Laugh track.

dressing (French and Italian) to the arrangement. The parents both sat down, as Carol, the daughter, joined them with a contemporary smile.

The Man Who Murdered Bowling
BY ROBERT TOWELL

FROM CHAPTER THIRTEEN:
BUILDING THE DEATH STAR IN SIX EASY STEPS

Somehow, through a loophole in the child labour laws of the late eighties, I switched parents. I was on the road so often that my parents began to sell my things and use my bedroom as a compost heap. They would send pictures (right to my trailer at the set), usually Polaroids, of my father dumping heaps of rhubarb stems and leaves and rotten zucchini onto what was once my bed. And, from the same set, or from the discomfort of my new foster home, there was a time that I wrote letters home, and when I say home I mean in the compost sense. Communication, I have always said, is essential in a domestic setting. I spent almost a year trying to communicate with the foster people where I lived, but it proved nearly impossible because they were usually eating or doing dental work on the neighbours. I lived with these uninspired foster folks during my last years of *Pumpkin Seeds*. I say uninspired because they only wore mauve, and ate celery that was chopped into giant chunks. It was everywhere, overwhelming and completely frustrating to see these giant wheel-sized pieces of celery in salads, soups, sandwiches, casseroles, even meat loaf. Those chunks seemed to just cry out *I cannot create anything, please kill me now*. However, a new entrepreneurial event unfolded before me.

In the very late eighties my foster parents had spearheaded the management position for me at the Mandarin buffet establishment at Yonge and Eglinton called Superior Mandarin where I worked on my days off from *Pumpkin Seeds*. It wasn't for me but I did the job for nine months, laying down the groundwork for my diplomacy and supreme dictatorship, and on weekends I would travel and try to work in the States.

While my foster parents didn't work much in the restaurant, they did play a key role in the business. We did use their help, quite often actually, to help boost our daily takes from the restaurant. What they did was paint it, which proved to be very clever.

They were brought in by the building manager and the chief operator of the Superior Mandarin franchise to assist in fuming the patrons, a technique that is very popular in Saskatoon and Gibralter. According to an article I read in *Fumes Quarterly*'s summer 1988 special, during peak hours, some restaurants would fume their patrons to enhance tips or to assist in the thinning of wallet contents.

My foster parents Cecil and Barbara were twice weekly painters and the higher-ups were fascinated with this prairie-Canadian dining technique. Fuming, as it was called, was when a restaurant was painted during peak hours and the cooks fanned out the cooking fumes from the kitchen and imported the paint fumes, then exported the confluence. Those dining who do not faint as a result of this toxic mix-up, usually become inebriated, and tip heavily. The unsuspecting clientele at a buffet can be monetarily generous. It was a bit of a kinky fetish, and a real ice-breaker for me and my fosters in a, *Hey, this is fun, knocking out patrons with paint fumes so we can rob them,* sort of way. So I would write my real mother from the restaurants after each heist, usually high as a kite myself.

November 1, 1990
Dear Son,

Do you like your new parents? I'm so sorry that you felt you couldn't trust me and your father with the news of your new-found television stardom. Things got so complicated, what with you away, and all those phone calls in the middle of the night from advertisers. We still watch the show up here but they say in the *TV Guide* that your character may be killed off. Why does everything always fall apart? Did you say something to the director? Are you not getting along with the crew? Does the show air on many channels in the States? How is filming going? Are you bullying everyone? I made a tuna fish sandwich here by accident, just as I was reading an interview with you, so now I know they are your favourites, at least that is what it says in *Teen Mist Monthly*. I didn't know you knew Kung-Fu! Or the tango for that matter. How exciting. We watch you each week on the fuzzy channel. Your little brother is washing his hair right now and he still loathes you, so it may be awkward at Christmas. How is your co-star Nikola? And your TV parents? I wish there was something I could do to help you Robert. You must believe that whatever you may have thought, I was only trying to work in your best interest. I was trying to see the real picture. We pushed you to bowl but it seems like television is your calling.

I remember when we were such good friends when you were little – going out to McDonalds after Nursery school.

Going shopping up at Bayview Village. How I used to sew and make your little clothes when you were napping. I'd better go before I get too mushy.

Love from your Mom.

June 8, 1991
Dear Mom,

The pastoral life is inherently unteleological: there is no ostensible beginning, no possible grand action, and therefore no real satisfactory ending except death and uncomforted mourning. Sound familiar? I tend in my life's work to move towards one generic situation, that of unhappy love, and so the viewer who recognizes the earmarks of my own testicular movement can find peace in knowing that failure is a form of birth control. I am emotionally violent and my fantasies are public. No, ironic as it may be, now in the grip of puberty I find myself masturbating while holding a framed photograph of my television mother doing laundry in her sexy white winter coat.

Well, it's that time of the year again when the postal workers give me those funny looks as I load their bags with tiny mechanical muffins armed with stamps and hearing aids. Yes, your birthday. I remember one of your birthdays and how much we tried our best to get you to the other side of the river. We were, in those days, deep in the urban parks of East York, the water was cold and you were afraid. There were no park rangers, just overturned garbage receptacles and Jeff had made a raft out of clay and I, out of birch from the same beautiful trees that were in the backyard at our first house on Mann Avenue, and we floated across the Serena Gundy river (even though you could never pronounce the name of the park properly, come on, Serena Gundy, it's easy) and cooked wieners and beans in the forest, brought them back to you and you ate them with jam. Then you bet all my money on middle-weight dog fights and I had to get another sitcom job in Guam. I had to get new parents as well and make plans to wed my television sister Nikola. I'm glad you can share it now in this letter, the warmth I know will keep you alive tonight as you lay in bed. I will be turning nineteen in nine months and I expect to grow three inches all over. When I am twenty-three you will be fifty-three.

I am quite depressed. The VCR is broken. I have bad credit so we can't sign a lease anywhere. Some women find men with money, others find me. Nikola says hello and hopes that you will be nice to our children in the coming decade or so. As for a poem or some sort of gift, the best I can do are these napkins from the Dairy Queen; unfortunately I had to use most of them on account of I smeared ice cream across my jaw as if I were applying a coat of varnish.

One time, when I *did* live at home and Jeff *was* my brother, we did a pantomime sketch, but with voices. We videotaped it. In one scene Jeff was ascending the stairs via a rope I tied to the banister. He said to me, (and this was all done improv) "Dad, why can't I just use the stairs?" and then he sniffed the rope and broke out of character and said, "Rob, this rope smells like varnish." Then it was my turn and the next shot was me, and I suspect Jeff was now filming. I took the rope and began to climb up the stairs, and then, using a Dad-like voice began to muddle my words and said, "Oh no, who put the varnish on it," and began to fall down the stairs to the floor. It was really funny but I guess what I'm saying is this letter is like the varnished rope. I must go as someone is filling up on tarty deserts by the catering cart I parked in front of my dressing room.

Life is a killer!

Robert Fucking Towell

July 1, 1991
Dear Son,

I don't remember the varnish vignette so well. How is your new place? I am sorry for withholding our new address, but we have adapted to you not being in our lives. I'm sure your new foster parents in Toronto will be a great learning experience for you.

How much money do you give your foster parents each month?

Love from Mom

July 3, 1991
Dear Mom,

I'm the manager of a restaurant. You and Dad and Jeff should come visit.

Love,
Robert Towell

On February 18, 1994, through a fax from my agent, I found out officially *Pumpkin Seeds* was not being picked up for an eighth season and that May 19 was the final taping. So I began to steal toilet paper and onion rings. Not just from the studio, but also from every fast food carnival I could find. At twenty-two I could hardly be considered an adolescent anymore. I told my agent I wanted out of television and to kindly molest actual under-aged clientele as I was tired of picking up the Denny's tabs for his insatiable desire for late night mashed potatoes and root beer. I remember, far too distinctly, the sandpaper texture of his fingertips along the exposed regions of my neckline as I exited the car. But I never thought things *in italics* back then like some nostalgic narratives, instead, I just inhaled the tailpipe fumes and headed home, ashamed, repressed, feeling as if I were being groomed for a life as a leading municipal park axe murderer on some eventual after school special sponsored by a leading acne cream manufacturer.

So yeah, the show was being cancelled. One of the first people I contacted that day was Billy Guthrie, my old bowling coach. It turned out that he had died earlier in the week when a pretzel truck backed over him in a parking lot during a routine empty gingerale bottle returning campaign. I remember the coach, constantly. His blurry and sparse red hair. I'd look for moral support but find my parents fist-fighting in the stands. So I would turn to where my coach was usually sitting but he'd be in the bathroom peeing gingerale. But I still won matches despite his absence. I just never assumed the beverage would become his life's work. Hearing of his death anchored me with carbonated fear, and even stranger still, at that moment, totally alone and devoid of provisions, I could taste an unscripted waft of stale gingerale caress my palette. The second person I contacted was Nikola's father but he wasn't home. I thought it was important, as I knew she was the one, to run the marriage plans by her father. Of course, I would have told him, had he been home, that it was a few years off, a good two years premature, but in those days I had a way of seeing the long and skinny of nuance. My fingers and voice were like a commanding stamp of approval with a very rich font, and a deep red stain with a rectangular border. Those of you who have spoken to me in person know this symbol as I'm sure it's burned into your psyche. In my experience, this insight is a feminine attribute. I am quite angelic. I save lives and for all intents and purposes, everything I say is a close cousin to the truth.

I was still three years from meeting Greg Lebelle and Dragan Momchilo, so I still had some time to enjoy my life outside of the legal system.

Nikola and I began to date heavily during the end of *Pumpkin Seeds* and I took her to Marineland in Niagara Falls. She told me that we would be married one day and I believed her. I drew her a map and told her to meet me in a food court of my choice on December 23, 1995. And she did. I told her I was going to intern at some major American manufacturing companies, drop out of school and mourn the loss of a close friend, but not necessarily in that order.

I was "hired" to work on the Brunswick catalogue. Brunswick is one of the leading American manufacturers of bowling equipment, and since I knew they would eventually be a big ally down the road, I wanted to make a good impression. My first assignment was to do promo copy for a new bowling bag. I remember sleeping with it the night before, well at least a sketch of it from a mock-up of the catalogue. And beside the sketch was a blank text box where my love letter would go. The only trouble was, I was feeling a truth serum, which is the only way I can describe it, a truth serum charging through my veins. I couldn't deny how I truly felt about bowling, maybe it was all the conversations with those who drew foul baths in the bowling culture that made me feel so unclean and ready to surrender ingenuity for a lifetime of stagnation. I'll never be sure, but for once in my life, I realized the power of the word, in its holiest sense, and I knew my duty went beyond promo copy. We were going to save lives.

BRUNSWICK DYNO RETRO SINGLE LEOPARD

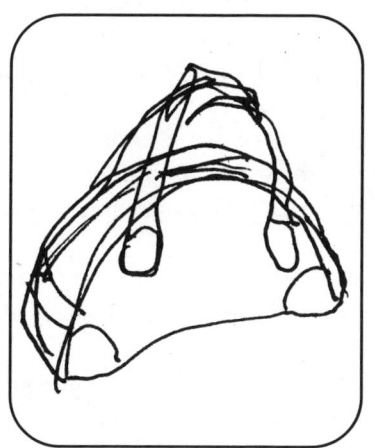

FEATURES:
single ball bag, retro style, holds ball & shoes up to size 9, foam ball rest

It's great to be morbid and stretch yourself vulnerable over the course of mythological necessity. The examination of truths stigmatizes the lower quarters of society. This trauma causes a socio-economic overspill or oversight, depending on ones accuracy. This overspill is eventually uprooted and becomes malignant and temperamental. So, treat yourself with Brunswick, the very best.

"FOR ONCE IN MY LIFE, I REALIZED THE POWER OF THE WORD, IN ITS HOLIEST SENSE, AND I KNEW MY DUTY WENT BEYOND PROMO COPY. WE WERE GOING TO SAVE LIVES."

— ROBERT TOWELL

WESTMOUNT, MONTREAL
SEPTEMBER 28, 1995

By now Robert Towell had settled into academic life, but the television brash still remained. He liked to make dressing rooms out of sections of his bedroom, and would often lock himself in the bathroom. Before segregating himself from his roommate, Clay Shallaghan, they recorded tracks for a possible album of thunderous theme songs under a thinly veiled corporate theme.

"Close the door, let's finish these tracks," commanded Robert Towell, who was fashioning a fluorescent toque and a red-knit sweater with the logo of a hockey stick etched diagonally across the chest. The duo had been discussing the reality behind academia: Robert felt betrayed that he had to pay for his textbooks, so he stalled on buying them altogether. Clay, who was studying music, specializing in sound engineering, was a lanky individual with a penchant for black beans and rice, and, by no choice of his own, had straw coloured hair, hazel eyes and thick lips that sought out a vocabulary of massive proportion.

Like other human beings, Clay's eyes and face were expressive. As some people's arms or eyes darted around with words, so did Clay's lips. His skin was oatmeal and his body hair was nearly translucent, causing him to appear, at times, slightly wolf-like.

That afternoon in the makeshift studio, the duo had achieved a great amount of bravado, laughter and joy despite the gummy aftergoo of the duct tape from the microphone stand.

They snapped some photos of their jam sessions; the flutters of brightness set off what some profess to be a semi-religious impulse that was not properly exorcised in his youth.

It wasn't until the taps stopped running that Clay Shallaghan realized Robert Towell had disappeared into the washroom. Noticing a sharp silence, and lack of sarcasm in the room, Clay continued to work, fiddling through some samples, trying to find a segment that resembled something between a frog and a bus.

"So, Robert, wanna work on another song?" He made his way to the closed bathroom door and spoke again. "Rob, what's wrong?" he asked. "You were fine an hour ago. Even five minutes ago."

"Nothing, I'm just inflating the mahogany arm rest so I am comfortable during these domestic interactions."

"No seriously, you've been in there for like ten minutes."

"Leave me alone, I have a bowling hangnail. When I come out I'm going to be a sports meanie."

"I'm out of here… ass wipe. And put my nail clippers and my toaster and badminton racket and cans of soup back when you're done with them."

"I need them," Robert replied, a pale monotone voice desperate for audience, garbled through the door. "I need all of them."

"Just put them back after," Clay said.

"Have fun, send me a postcard. I'll be in here," Robert said. "Deep in the recesses."

The Man Who Murdered Bowling
BY ROBERT TOWELL

FROM CHAPTER FIFTEEN: PAPERCLIPS ARE NOT WEAPONS OF MASS DESTRUCTION

It was early October, 1995. I was deflating some orphaned office pastries six days into my internship with Brunswick, having quit University for life, or rather, for a life in the real world. For some unholy reason, the branch was located in Ohio, and boasted the fastest fact checkers and most loyal copy editors for the country's lead-

FROM WHAT WE'VE BEEN TOLD, TOWELL WAS A SEAMLESS PRANKSTER. ONE NIGHT AT HINGSTON HALL YOU AWOKE FROM HAVING A NIGHTMARE OF A GIRL WITH SMALL HANDS. AFTER INITIAL CONSOLING, DID TOWELL GO OUT AND BRING HOME A SMALL-HANDED GIRL?

Clay: Robert always had a way of showing compassion at the wrong time. He did, in fact, bring back this girl. It was, for him, a gesture of friendship, you know, that he really knew me and could provide some wholesome comfort and nurturing to me in a needful time. She was high strung and kept punching me and trying to get me to go make her breakfast. What's more is that she looked exactly like the girl in my nightmare. Like I said, classic bad timing on his part.

CLAY, WHERE DID THE "JUPITER SHUFFLE" COME FROM? CAN YOU ACT OUT A BIT OF THE MOVE FOR US?

Clay: Good question! The full answer would require a lengthy dissection of Robert Towell's mental make-up, personality, behaviour and motives which would take time and would compromise the interests of a man who stills sends the occasional bone my way. Lemme see… well in the early years when I first met Towell he was a bit muddled on the issue of the real and imagined, the physical and the ethereal, kinetic energy and potential energy and so on. He had a shameless devotion to building an imaginary kingdom or community in his head populated with "real life" figures such as friends and family.

Like most kingdoms there was a king and below that a hierarchy of lords and servants, angels and demons. In short he was living in his head and would not concede his orgiastic fantasies to the unglamorous reality of his declining mental and physical health, and the collapse of his newly minted corporation. To his credit his fantasy was vast, colourful, full of sex and hot tub action. Quite charming if you were a lord in this kingdom but ice-cold if you were a servant. Again I must say that this confusion was also his wisdom... I mean look where we are now with *WCB* due to the sheer force of this megalomaniac ego.

Anyway this head-trip started to get tedious, like a bad tv show, and ratings were down, let me tell you. He became difficult and unbearable to his small retinue of remaining associates. He had taken to always carrying around a bit of trash in his clenched fists and yelling things like *"you work for me,"* to the strangers in malls and small businesses. He was unkempt and smelled like old roast beef. Someone had to step in, and at that time it was me. I thought that if I could interrupt the flow of his dream world with some recognition of physical reality this could only be a healing vector. I taught Robert to dance that winter by telling him we were shooting a video for his song *"Faith"* and put a mirror in front of him. Soon the mirror was gone and he was dancing in public places with other people. Some of these people were of the opposite sex and some of them were dancing too. Well, the inner-drama took a back seat to this new physical celebration. It was a great pleasure for me at first to watch

ing supplier of bowling equipment. I'll be honest, I was hyped at my desk, facing my computer screen as my third coffee raced through me.

The meagre office held a pungent scent of staples and factory pulp up to my aging nostrils. I had spent the better part of the morning sketching bowling shoes, as I had some ideas that I wanted to pitch to Reebok and Nike. All in good time, I thought. I stared at the copy in front of me, my first assignment, as if I was the Moses of bowling, trying to channel something bigger, and save the faceless masses. Don't shoot the messenger, I thought, kneading my feet into the rotten carpet that housed no less than three different races of therma-beetles, a popular domestic species in the greater Ohio region. I could go on, but really, this was a big day in the whole bowling revenge plot. So I was reading my version of the copy.

My supervisor and catalogue editor, Gary Stedman, had been moaning all week about how he had been staying up late looking over the proofs for the winter issue that was due to hit the world in November.

The heavy-set boss in the pleated pants who held the dented pen cap to his lips and chewed aggressively re-read my contribution since I had just left the final copy of my draft in his mailbox.

Though he was a good seventeen feet away, I deduced his body odour was a confluence of week-old beets and fabric softener. I crooked my neck and caught his stance, holding my copy and scratching his facial growth with concern. He had no hair, it was just a sweaty atmosphere that helmeted around his bulbous skull. As he looked at the words, I could tell old Gary knew he was staring into the face of insanity.

The ceiling fan purred away, and like a constant leather tongue in the late autumn heat, it dampened my already puzzled spirit. I had a devilish second melee with the custodian in the hallway, something about after dinner mint accidents and the lack of decent pastries in the neighbourhood. I was also promised by the administration to be given the antidote to thwart the fax machine. Its cord was a tail, and I'm sure, alone at night, it caterwauled a hostile shriek that toppled file folders and caused the common tea bag to burst into flame.

I returned to my desk, studying the memo about the fax machine, when I noticed old Gary Stedman muffining his way towards my desk. Poor bastard, he had no idea about re-hydration, was getting too much salt and starch, getting puffy and looked like all he ate was sand.

"Something wrong Mr. Stedman? You look concerned."

him grow and discover and reach out to other dancers, myself included. I remember once we were dancing and with uncompromised boyish enthusiasm he looked at me and yelled: "It helps my glands!" That was his way of thanking me. Now to answer your question. One night at one of our popular spots called The Jupiter Room we were dancing and Robert was really quite randy. He was trying to "score with hos" as he would say, much to my chagrin, and he was really dancing expressively. I was in my expressive mode too and was attracting the attention of a number of the young women on and off the floor. I noticed that Robert kept bumping in to me and passing in front of me and it became quite apparent that Robert was trying to "score my swag" so to speak, trying to redirect the attention of my flock of female consorts his way. Well I watched with great sadness and pity as he danced back and forth in front of me with his arms like this *[demonstrates a blocking motion]* trying to cover me and steal my fire. What more can I say about that, it's a character sketch in itself... sad really.

"Wrong?" Gary Stedman said waving my copy. "Robert, it makes no sense. Not little sense, NO SENSE." Stedman threw the page into the air in front of my desk.

"What's wrong with that?" I asked.

"It's supposed to be an ad for a bowling bag, a brief ditty for the person using the equipment, not a sermon about… whatever you've written.

"Fatality. It's about fatality."

Just then a gust of liquid paper fumes throttled my senses and I became agitated. I felt guilty, like I was perhaps wasting Gary's time.

"It's the work of a foaming loon!" he snapped.

"Maybe a loon," I considered, "but not one who foams. The common people, yes they might be fooled by the pseudo-illusory quality, but not, let's say, a doctor. *This* copy makes sense to a doctor."

"Maybe your doctor," Gary replied, arching an eyebrow, causing some dead skin to float off and land somewhere on my desk. I saw my vision was once again being compromised. I began clawing at pieces of paper at my desk all the while staring at good ol' Gary. I asked him nicely, "Who'd you rather have buying your equipment? John the manager at Frippy's Meats or Dr. Sandy Meijers?"

"I'm not running this in our catalogue," Gary said with dictatorial finality.

"Fine, I'll make my own damn merchant's catalogue and cut you out," I said, standing up, gathering my kennel of stationary and giving those in the office a series of glares.

"But you're an intern here; it's your job to follow our routines and technical requirements."

"Maybe that's your policy, but

I'm trying to find out first hand how to sell bowling to the masses."

Frustrated and possessed, I was soon on a bus back to Canada, to find Nikola, my estranged ex-sister and future wife, who in a matter of hours I would begin courting, from nipple to nostril, for I, Robert Towell knew that it would be the strongest love.

He shaved with the foam shaving cream in between large bites of tofu-fried rice. Toy army man sized helmets of green peas were found in the hefty mouthfuls. The food court was dense with laughter and sneaker traffic, and as he shoveled and shaved, Robert Towell watched the blurry custodian push some carrots on the food court floor with a dirty mop. He thought: *I am not enjoying this shave, not at all.* He changed his disposition as the first toes of Nikola came into view, her pencil skirt worn a little too tight, making her walk slightly strained through the stiff plastic chairs. Her light blue blouse was the same colour as the ocean but also as the food she was about to eat. Maybe that's why she liked it, a lunch break vacation in her mouth. Nikola returned slowly from the frozen yogurt counter with something light blue in her mouth. *I ate a Smurf,* she thought to herself. *Is that a good one? Would Robbie like it? This looks good.* She took a big bite from her red spoon. She was wearing heels and it showed.

Robert tilted his neck as far back as it would go until he felt the bone's seam. His bright baby-blue shirt with its freshly ironed crisp collar bladed out from his subtle grey blazer, his gold ring and bracelet made his hand rattle against the table, and as he watched the mop tentacles drag themselves over the custodian's shoelaces, there was one thought: *I have jet black hair.* Then, his mental vanity propelled itself into cliff diving focus and broke on the table in front of him bravely. Without a granule of regret Robert spoke, "Her only love is me."

He had not seen Nikola in over a year, not including a stopover in Atlanta when they were doing a commercial together and had dinner. At this dinner Robert made the mistake of ordering the non-existent three-hooker salad.

In another world theirs was a daily interaction, tailor-made for seamless hours of mutual discovery and hibernation, Robert and Nikola had been inseparable. Then, like most unions they were ripped apart, detoured and unresolved, their paths spun out of control. They were like a ripped bus transfer sullied into a pulpy soup by the rain, illegible and expired.

No, not this time, Robert Towell said to himself, there would be more than an airport meal served by mental midgets in orange bibs with self-righteous acne and the pompous glow of a rapist dental hygienist. No, this

IN THOSE EARLY YEARS, PRIOR TO THE FORMATION OF WORLD CHAMPIONSHIP BOWLING, ROBERT TRIED HIS HAND AT SEWING AND MANUFACTURING HIS OWN MERCHANDISE. HOW DID HE FARE?

Nikola: Though Robert began working in a purely corporate framework, his addiction to the illusion of his own masterful talent caused him to try a variety of obscure crafts. He was ashamed of his failure in the shoe manufacturing industry, which to this day he cannot reconcile. He attempted to start a wide-scale underwear manufacturing unit through an illusory Berlin connection, which sadly failed to materialize due to enormous manufacturing costs. Each pair retailed for twelve dollars but required a minimum of ten dollars in material costs, twelve hours in labour and no fewer than four drumming children and sometimes as many as three dominatrix per two workers.

But shoe making was Robert's dream.

Bowling shoes required little to no talent in the manufacturing process. Much like the sport itself the shoe had an unimpressive appearance and did not fit properly.

WHEN DID YOU KNOW TOWELL WAS THE ONE FOR YOU?

Nikola: There have been many moments during which I have known that Robert should not be the one for me. Unfortunately he is. It is not amusing that I find his obsessive corporatization of life endearing. When we first lived together, I criticized his uselessly compulsive shoe making and fabric sewing. Soon after I confronted him he quit. It was strange for him to do something so unself-involved. I was thinking of starting a sort of portable spa for women executives, you know, take your girls on a weekend getaway, give them nice underwear and pamper them. It's the way I want to be treated, and I think people will pay for that service.

meeting would be something concrete from concentrate. It would transcend empty times apart and be as potent as before. Not since their television days — those seven long seasons under the heat of studio lamps — would they so congeal and bloom into a great fiscal return to form. *Now,* he thought, now he had her back, her blue eyes and snarling smile and high-piled blonde hair that alarmed any bakery, stationary store or hotel conference. They were a team again and nothing would stop them. Not even if the custodian sprouted prehistoric fangs, turned assassin and from his dirty bucket began throwing pruning sheers. No, nothing would stop this corporeal wet dream, this brick by brick installation, this corporation of the heart.

Though high-strung and sometimes careless, he was a bit sappy and even nostalgic. He had all her letters on file, samples of her hair from her dressing room — there was still a connection, a convincing undeniable connection. He shaved away the final section of foam and rinsed off with a wet-nap.

"Her only love is me," Robert Towell cackled. He caught his reflection, this time in the napkin dispenser.

"Who are you talking to?" Nikola said, sitting down. She took another bite, this time daintily. "It's cold."

"No one Nikola. Now, how long have we been together, would you estimate?"

"About eight years?"

"Well, isn't it time we put our corporate dreams to work?" Robert said with a smile. He downed another steaming spoonful of rice, and snuck a few peanuts onboard.

"What's that? You know I might be starting up my accessory line," she said sketching on a napkin.

"Really? That's great. Because I have something to tell you."

"What is it Robbie?"

"Look, I think I found out what I really want to do for the next three years tops."

"What is that?" Nikola said, and began to rub the top of Robert's hand.

"Did I ever tell you about my parents?" Robert said, taking his hand back and running it across his jaw.

"No."

"I mean, my real parents. Not those idiots on the show with us. And not those fosters either."

"Yes, I know who you are talking about. That is, I knew you weren't referring to the actors."

"Well, let's see," Robert began. "I don't know exactly how to start this," he paused, taking her hand with physical and dramatic punctuation. "I've repressed a lot of this so it may sound as if I'm lying, at least to me it may sound this way."

"God Robert, just spit it out," Nikola said, tonguing her spoon.

"A year before I got cast for *Pumpkin Seeds* it was the end of this huge run in my life, this sports sweat shop run."

"You're insane."

"Yes, yes I am. But I was really good at something."

"What was that? Being crazy?"

"It was disgusting really. I mean, the stink of it all, like a foul dead cartoon bird that rots, that no one sees but you. I really don't know if I can talk about it and still look you in the eyes. I mean, I was a kid so I didn't know any better."

"What was it?"

"I got trophies, a whole den full of them I was so good."

"Okay Robbie, just tell me what you were so good at before you were cast and got trophies for, enough trophies to fill a den."

"And some in the hallway too."

"And the hallway."

"Bowling."

"What?"

"I was a child bowling superstar. I mean, it wasn't like I was exploited on a farm, or made shoes for telethon hosts, but I've never told anyone this, I mean, I was used."

"What's the big deal?" Nikola said, looking down at her ample dose of cleavage. "You played a sport, so what?"

"It's just a part of my past that I've had to hide."

"Why have you hidden it?"

"It's too painful."

"Robert, let's confront reality… together."

"I have. That's the problem."

"Why haven't you ever talked about this, if it bothered you so much?"

"Well, mainly for mental and legal reasons. You see Nikola, darling, everyone who knew I was a bowler when I was seven is now dead. I never really thought about it. Until now. Now I know what I have to do."

"Dead?"

"Look, I'm exaggerating, if only to make a point."

"Rob, you're freaking me out, what does this have to do with our corporate dreams?"

"I'm glad you asked Nikola. But before I continue, let me just say that I really want to have sex on this food court table."

"Well, that's nice, but we would get arrested."

"Yes, we would. I could take a photograph of this food court table, and somehow manifest it in my apartment and then achieve today's sexual goal."

"Or we could just do it in the washroom."

"Yes, yes we could."

They laughed and finished their food. Her question was answered, their corporate dreams addressed as they juggled their accounts and began to put order to their economic galaxy. Together they had earned a good sum of money from *Pumpkin Seeds*, and most of this money still existed. Robert continued, stroking her soft hand.

"I was going to go to law school, but who needs it?"

32

"Well, it still might be an option for you."

"I did six weeks of media at university and hated it, law school would be even worse."

"So together we have this much." Nikola slid the calculator across the table. Robert glanced at the result.

"No one knows a thing about my life." Robert finished up his last chew of rice.

"What about *Teen Mist Magazine*? They seem to know you."

"I rest my case, Your Honour."

"What do you mean no one knows a thing about your life?"

Napkin sketch by Nikola.

"I can come and go as I please."

"Would you stop talking like that, it's too disconnected from what is happening now. Now is this table and this calculator and this plan. Nothing more," Nikola said in a stern voice. "Are we going to go walk up the mountain? You promised we'd go in the snow."

"Nobody knows me. Nobody knows me. Nobody knows me." Robert continued murmuring the words in a trance that lasted close to ten minutes before Nikola put her fingers into his mouth, something she had done before, although usually when Robert was asleep. This, she said, stopped him from snoring or making barfing noises.

Huddled together, they took the mountain slowly, and looked across the city. There was the defunct imperfection of Olympic Stadium and a not too distant bridge where Casinos had made their mark on the face of Montreal. Somewhere south existed the Rose Bowl in all its Bethlehemic glory. Somewhere, deep in the recesses of his own lucid mind, Robert ignited this experience, enlarged it, and made it feel like corduroy in his palms. He cupped Nikola's young breasts under her coat and pulled her down into the snow with him. The mountain melted at their touch.

WORLD CHAMPIONSHIP BOWLING HEADQUARTERS

TORONTO, ONTARIO
FEBRUARY 15, 1996

Robert and Nikola Towell giddily unpacked the stationary and plugged in the microwave in their new staff room. The couple had been married the night before in a private ceremony in Niagara Falls, the Las Vegas of Ontario. The ceremony was videotaped, and witnessed only by the minister and an off-key organist. They did Jell-O shots off cleavage in the wax museum, and carried on well into the hour of the whore.

Robert was opening up his mail, a plethora of bowling journals and magazines. After absorbing the general idea, he threw them into the shredder, which he had just plugged in. A fax from a toy manufacturer came in, as well as a recent consumer survey that Jerry Tomlin had orchestrated at local malls. "These are great," he told Nikola who scurried in and out of the WCB office.

"What's great?" Nikola asked.

"Jerry's survey; the answers are really compelling. I think this will help us shape the marketing campaign."

What the survey revealed was as follows: When asked what specifically they disliked about televised bowling 74% answered how slow the bowlers moved combined with their lack of personality; 21% said it was the clothing and the haircuts; 5% said the way it was shot made it boring; 67% of respondents thought bowling was boring on television and never stopped while flipping. When shown the WCB logo and promotional material 84% of respondents thought the logo was eye catching compared to the leading competition. Sports that people enjoyed watching or playing were as follows: 36% hockey, 21% soccer, 14% basketball, 11% baseball, 9% bowling, while 2% preferred lawn bowling.

Robert put the survey material down and ripped open more mail, a newsletter from local businesses offering cleaning services as well as bulk mail from the Professional Bowler's Association with its coma inducing script.

"Even their journalism is boring. I'm sorry, but I think God wants me to do this."

"Do what Rob?" Nikola asked, arranging a plant in the lobby.

"Oh, you know," Robert snarled, opening a pack of thumbtacks.

When Robert Towell came in from the cold he did not remove his jacket until he had ordered a gin and tonic. The building was low-lit, small, with a few tables and a juke box near the bar. Robert Towell was wearing a pastel grey blazer with a shiny purple shirt underneath, its collar shark-like. He moved silently through the room until he was within earshot of a giant man who skulked in front of the cigarette machine. He watched the giant move in front of the pool tables, and stare down into the green felt void, sighing heavily.

"Are you playing a game? Waiting for someone?" Robert Towell asked the man, whose details were unique. Towell thought he resembled a gargoyle, a pacing gargoyle. The gargoyle huffed, sighed, his eyes never blinking. As Robert approached the young man there was dedication in the reciprocating movement. This man understood.

"No. Well, yeah, I want to play. Fuck," the gargoyle responded. Towell thought, *This guy is really animated, such a crazy energy I get from him, some sort of protection, a weird mascot of strength, aggression, adrenaline, and sex.*

"Want to play a quick game?" Robert Towell asked.

"Sure."

"My name is Robert."

"I'm Greg."

"Good to meet you. How's your day going?"

The man's face was crimped in stiff pain. "Okay."

"You sure? You look like you're in pain."

"Just a bit sore. I had sex a couple of nights ago for the first time in two months. I'm still sore."

"I understand."

"Well, the reason is, I had surgery recently. I lost one of my testicles to cancer, doctors said I'd be infertile. Next thing I know I got this chick pregnant."

"You showed them," Robert Towell said with a strange half-smile. He was enjoying the afternoon, thinking about this man's crashing energy that came in big frozen waves which made him shudder. It wasn't the temperature in the bar, it was not the weather outside, or a lack of sleep. Towell later recalled the meeting with much affection, saying: "I'm not sure what exactly transpired, but I knew that this man would be in my

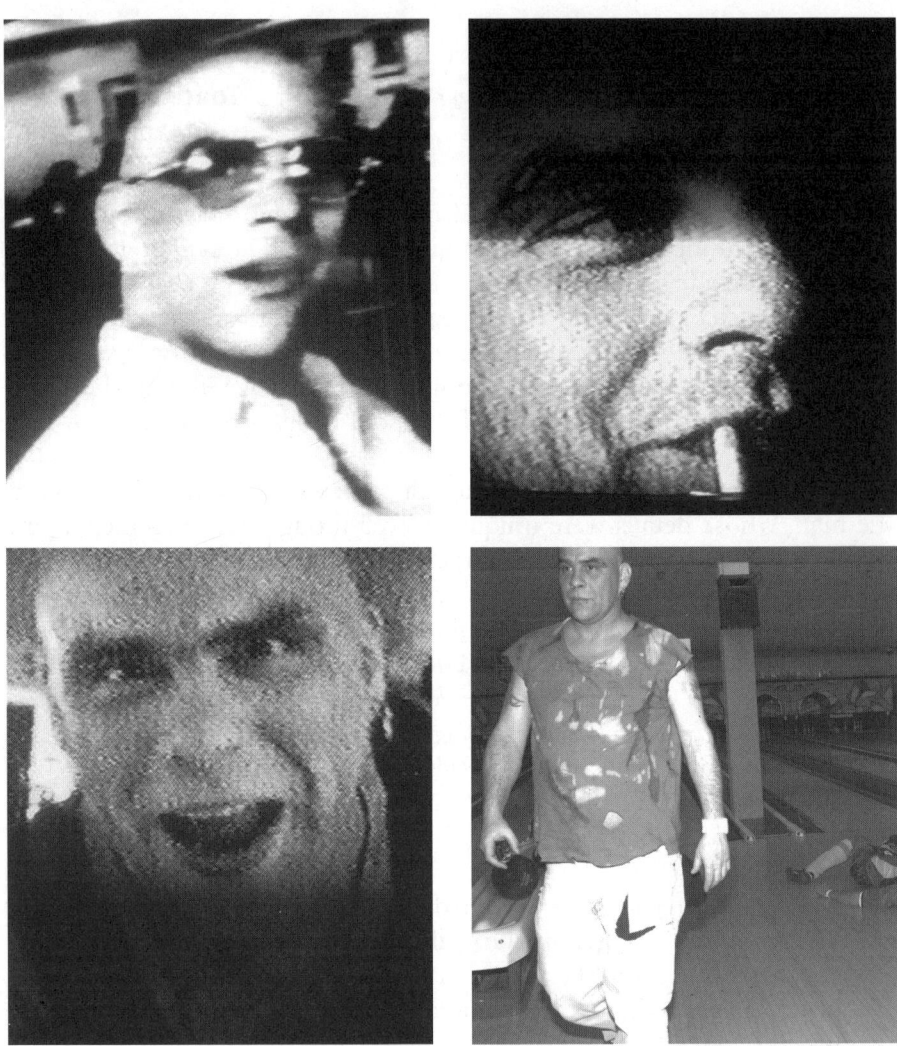

Icons of bowling's evolution: *Greg Lebelle (circa 1996) represented the new bowling hero; (circa 1997) the bully character ushered in the Lebelle / Momchilo feud; (circa 1998) Lebelle runs wild at a title defense; (circa 1999) Lebelle paves the way for the late night pay-per-view extreme bowling era.*

life, my thoughts, and my paperwork for the rest of my life. There was some unsavoury element about him that I could market, that I could control, or at least, I thought I could. I'm sure most people just have friendships, and that works for them. I just have this artificial gene, one that turns people into cardboard. Call me old fashioned."

After playing three games they exchanged phone numbers and parted ways, into the lake of noise that awaited both men in the late afternoon.

In the diabetic afternoon, when cardboard weakened in the sun, the youthfully European Dragan Momchilo had finished his soccer game with four goals. He made his way to the bus stop where Robert Towell watched him from behind the gas station which overlooked a mall.

"Fuck, where the hell is it?" the young man whined. He was prone to panic and began to mutter and curse as he retraced his steps in the smelly parking lot. He carried his soccer equipment in one hand, while the other waved a lit cigarette. He walked towards the mall but turned down into the bowling alley with sudden speed. Towell knew what was down there, he also knew the underground complex was a smoking zone where the athlete would not be fined or maimed.

Robert followed the boy, who, though European in the physical sense, was a lot like him, a by-product of capitalism, mass culture and 7-11.

It was this reflection he saw in Dragan, his own perhaps, that drew him in, for there was no definable quality that could be lifted after years of dissection.

Later, Robert would admit behind closed corporate doors, that the young man's personality was inconsistent at best and his strongest virtue was his willingness for physical exertion.

But initially, it was a gelling, the brotherhood of their urban hedges, playing in dirty water parks and knee scrapes that still stung in the rain, the obvious boy-dom origin that bonded them;

WAS THERE ANY INDICATION THE PUBLIC WOULD BE INTERESTED IN THIS OR DID YOU THINK IT WAS JUST A JOB?

Dragan: It was more of a passion. Robert Towell had commercials lined up for every type of person you could imagine, every demographic. Balding overweight kids who couldn't get dates, pregnant teenage wives... He even wanted to do a spot where we'd shave kids' heads in the playground and shove donuts down their throats to demonstrate some sorta bowler fat farm that parents should worry about. Apparently, Towell was then going to show kids in good shape working out under the supervision of his own bowling utopia. Greg (Lebelle) shaved his head and just by coincidence looked like a mutated Mr. Clean. He even had the earring. I tried to deny being a bowler but it would come into my dreams, and the shame of my father was overwhelming. He was an international sports figure; it was in my blood, no matter how hard I tried to run from it.

simply put, they were cut from the same plastic straw. Sensing the potential to see even deeper into his own loathsome self, Towell crawled from behind his bunker of mischief.

"I remember that moment well," recalls Towell. "I looked at Dragan shrinking in the distance as the building swallowed him up, and then, looking at the name above the entrance, *Bowlerama*, it sent a shiver down my spine, and I thought, yes, I must follow him, deep into the suburban lungs of this giant whale."

Downstairs, in the decayed open-heart of the bowling alley, where the lights reflected the sour grease-yellow paint job, Towell watched the boy struggle with his bag of soccer gear as he pawed for payphone change. He began to choke, not prepared for the tributaries of sweat and stale smoke that made his eyes water.

Robert Towell recalls: "I remember Dragan was lighting a cigarette and began scratching his head as if Morse code was eminent. I slowed down as I passed him at the payphone, and when he spoke he had this distinct phlegm gargle, a voice which cradled the sound of his words. I wanted to strangle the phlegm out of his ignorant throat, as if he was a farm animal resistant to evolving. I'll be honest, it was creepy, or I was being creepy, but when you get an idea, when you put your mind to something, no amount of self-consciousness can really cause you to wimp out in some sort of doomed school yard doubt fever. I knew what I needed at that moment."

The young man was terrified, pacing and inhaling and puckering the air for an answer. After a great deal of pacing, someone picked up on the other end of the line.

"Finally, Jesus, Mom. Can you put Nick on the phone, I have to get him to check my room for my wallet."

Meanwhile, Robert Towell made his way over to the main desk of the Thorncliffe Bowlerama. He was sweating now.

"I found this wallet, there's ID in it," Towell said, turning his head to the boy on the payphone.

The smell of freshly cut fries and hairspray was undeniable to all in range. This was just the beginning, Towell thought. This was the beach, the untapped beach of a lost civilization.

"Never mind, I think it's him," Towell said, pretending to be astonished while comparing the image on a piece of photo ID with the man on the phone. The young man gushed with relief when Towell held up the wallet.

"Is it yours?" Robert Towell asked, surveying the building with a cautious eye. The building made him sick, but he was strong.

Icons of bowling's evolution: *Dragan Momchilo (circa 1995) with soccer in his blood; (circa 1996) the babyface arrives at BOWLFEST; (circa 1997) "Hollywood" Dragan Momchilo cuts a powerful WCB promo; (circa 1999) moonlighting sports icon in full insanity gear.*

"I hope so."

"Looks like you. Found it upstairs in the parking lot."

"Thanks mister. Fuck, I thought I lost it."

"I know what it's like to lose something. It feels bad. Like cancer."

"You've had cancer?"

"No, not exactly, if you want to know why I said that, it's because I've been thinking about this friend of mine."

"Oh, well thanks for finding this. Sorry about your friend."

"You play soccer here a lot?"

"Not here," Dragan said, looking around and snorting in disgust.

"No, I mean, you were playing earlier, on the field down the street?"

"Yeah, I play every Tuesday."

"That's great," Robert said, offering the best smile he could muster despite the bowling flashbacks coming on heavy, and in no predictable order. He felt uneven knots being tied in his stomach, he was sweating, and pacing back and forth.

"I have to go, but thanks again."

"Maybe you want to play for my team sometime?"

"You have a soccer team?"

"No, this is a different kind of team, television-oriented. Lots of choreography, and conceptual integrity."

"I don't understand what you are saying."

"I know. Here's my number. You should call me on Tuesday."

Dragan Momchilo walked out of the bowling alley as Robert picked up the payphone and clunked a quarter into the slot. After a few rings a smile split across his face. "Hey Jerry, yeah it's me Rob."

"What's new, haven't heard from you in a..."

"I know," Towell cut him off. "I've figured it all out. So, meet me at the office next week, you're starting full time."

"It went well?"

"Yes it did, I think I can round up a roster in the next three days, it's really easy actually. I need you to keep your eye on this guy who plays soccer in Thorncliffe Park, every Tuesday. I'll send you his photo and I know what you're going to say, I don't know, I just have a hunch."

"Yeah boss," Jerry Tomlin replied. "Whatever you say."

Jerry Tomlin hung up, as did Robert Towell. There was work to be done; looking confident was part of their mantra. More thoroughbred than clotheshorse, but enough horse to win the race, is what they would say with a chorus of gin laughs. Later would come the heat of the first summer of pro bowling's howling surgery.

B y now Robert Towell had convinced several small businesses to spon-sor his first pay-per-view event, BOWLFEST.

"He was really calculating and charismatic," said Jerry Tomlin, who worked closely with Towell for the first half of 1996, until he demanded a paycheque. "We'd worked most mornings without a break, it was constant chatter, phones, faxing, crunching numbers and booking meetings."

Now that the project had moved out of the start-up Toronto office and onto the wide open Niagara Falls strip, Towell's confidence swelled.

He was of course, impeccably groomed, wearing subtle pastels. His cuticles were clean enough to eat off. He wore boxer-briefs, unable to totally shed himself of one trend or the other.

It was a late lunch financed by some well-invested sitcom earnings that allowed World Championship Bowling owner Robert Towell to watch the large businessmen slurp their spaghetti at Pompeii lava speed.

Now halfway through his first glass of ice water, Robert Towell regarded his clientele with acute disgust. The partial-hogs swaddled in spaghetti gestured to Towell with a series of encouraging movements and nostril grunts. This fuelled Towell to order more water, and to give several inches more between himself and the clients. And then just as the carbohydrate deluge seemed to subside, another round of heated grain found its way lipside. Robert Towell was puzzled, but more angry than puzzled. Rituals, he thought, were a waste of fucking time. Eating, sleeping, breathing were all dead arts. He was completely put off his food, but the business would get done. He was patient.

Robert waited until he was finished his own food before speaking. It wasn't an effective technique. If Robert Towell had really wanted their attention, he would have needed to hold up a large napkin engulfed with flames, because their dedication to the food was religious. His eyes scanned the men, but they were not looking. He wanted them to notice his intention to begin the meeting. He hated talking and eating at the same time. He said, "This is the way for you folks, meeting and eating and talking."

The two locals from the downtown strip drank beer with their pasta and nodded, grabbing rolls of bread from passing waitresses and downing plenty of butter, plastic cups and all. It was true, the men seemed to indicate with their eyes, this was the way for them.

Beside Robert Towell sat Greg Lebelle, a man, he had once remarked, who "has his own atmosphere." The friendly beast was then a 33 year old ex-everything: dealer, crew leader, stripper, and in the early eighties, even the occasional adult movie star. He and his twin brother Richard were orphaned in September 1963, and grew up in New Brunswick.

To imagine his name at birth, Arthur McGillis, on the bill of a WCB program was near-impossible.

At sixteen, a jagged Lebelle headed west to Edmonton and was a clever thief. Finally landing in Toronto in the mid-eighties, he sobered up and started a lucrative wholesaling business before the company, Lebelle Enterprise Inc., went bankrupt after three years. The following year, his estranged brother turned up in Toronto, gay and cancer-ridden. It was twenty years earlier on a hilltop when Richard told Greg about his orientation after the two brothers had decided to run away together. Greg Lebelle, unable to cope, punched his brother out and ran off. For him, Richard's death was impossible to take on the inside. He would later explain, "For the first sixteen years of my life, I spoke in first person plural, everything started with 'We', and then, fuck," Lebelle said, getting choked up, "I turned my back on him, forever."

Robert Towell had learned a lot about his new franchise bowling star on their ride in from Toronto. Towell would later explain from an undisclosed location: "The fall-out with his twin and the misery-laden events that would shape their horrible Toronto reunion in the late eighties was a key to his adult identity. Confronting yourself is one thing, but confronting yourself, watching yourself die in front of you, your half, no man should have to witness that, but he did, and survived. You don't just dust yourself off and walk away from that. The shattered fraternity he fell from, so personal, so tragic, and internal, yet its imprint is clearly visible."

Greg Lebelle carefully watched the businessmen's faces, and watched Robert watching their faces and watched the waitresses pouring coffee and stretching limbs. He studied the hem of her dress then returned his stare to their table; he knew he had a job to do.

Lebelle watched and inhaled. He watched because Robert Towell wanted him to watch, he wanted him to be there, to have his back, on this, the first sponsorship meeting. This was how it would be. Towell listened as they tried to string words together in between piping bites of bread. He could tell by the tone of their voices that he would be required to speak.

"So, are you ready to talk business, the future of sports sponsorship, or what?" Towell said with a sideways glance at the restaurant. Lebelle backed him up in silence.

"What exactly do you have in mind, it's a boxing match inside a bowling alley?"

"No, not at all. It's full contact bowling. Weapons, pyrotechnics, hyper-play-by-play, cutting edge graphics, bowlers with real personalities, who take risks, prevent each other from scoring, knock their opponents down and then throw gutters when its not their turn, you know so it's like, the computer thinks the guy gets a zero for that round."

"Sounds wild."

"And it's not just fighting, I mean, there is still bowling, it's just there are different types of matches. We're planning on expanding some of the general principles of bowling, having run-ins, storylines involving girl-friends, we are even having some martial arts experts come in and train some of the bowlers."

These men, sleazily dressed local businessmen in their middle-class utopia, had agreed to meet Robert Towell after three rounds of near convincing: faxing, phone conferences and a hail of well-stamped postcards.

"WCB's mandate is to change bowling forever, improve it. In my league, there is no such thing as an illegal pinfall. That rule is out, so any pin knocked down in an illegal manner, such as by a pinsetter, a ball bouncing off the rear cushion, or a ball that bounces in and out of a channel, is legal. I'm also toying with the number of frames. Ten sounds like a lot. Maybe five frames. And also, the size of the balls. I mean, five or ten pin, whatever you like. In golf they get to pick club sizes. That's another technical advantage of my version of bowling. All I want is for a few thousand regular bowling viewers to see what WCB is doing and say, yeah, I like that, before they turn the channel."

To Towell and Lebelle these local merchants seemed dyed in stress and age. "They were really boring, I wanted to die that afternoon," Towell confessed. Lebelle agreed: "It was just routine, we had to get that first sponsor, the food was okay, and I got to go to the Criminal Hall of Fame on the way home."

Finally at around 4:30, Robert Towell watched as all parties crossed that subtle bridge between supply and demand, known to most as the tablecloth, and as they all stuffed their faces with carbohydrates, peppering their words with coughs, grunts, and primal nods, the sly bowling gangster tried to trap them in his plot.

"Look, you sponsor my first three shows, and then I give you an option to sponsor us for the rest of our run on top at a very reduced rate. Plus you can carry some of our merchandising, and we will even do in-store appearances, we're talking huge PR. Commercial spots too; you have no idea, this is going to blow up."

"What do you mean the rest of your run on top?"

"This is Greg Lebelle," Towell said with rejuvenation. "Imagine him holding your chains on screen, in front of the sports complexes we'll dominate, come on you know it'll work."

"You sound like you've worked out all the bugs, I mean, it's fresh, but I don't know if it's for us," a man named Jim said.

"But Jim, it's tough, hardware's tough. I mean, I think it's cohesive," his colleague suggested.

"SPORTS HAS REACHED THE LOWEST COMMON DENOMINATOR. IT'S CEREAL BOXES AND BOX SCORES. IT'S STEROID SCANDAL AND RAPE TRIALS. IT'S ABOUT SELLING JUICE AND DEODORANT. NAMING BUILDINGS AFTER OBESE MILLIONAIRES. TEAMS ARE OBSESSED WITH THEIR BUILDINGS. THEY NAME THEM. OWN THEM. PROFIT INSIDE THEM. WE WILL HAVE NO HOME. ALL WE WILL HAVE IS THIS, EACH OTHER. THIS IS REAL."

— ROBERT TOWELL

"It'll be fine, you'll see. No one is doing this, we just need some sponsors to get things going," Towell explained.

"But we're a hardware store."

"Yes so?"

"So how is our product going to be helped by sponsoring your sports show? And you haven't even told us what sport it is?"

Seamlessly, Robert padded on compliments thick like therapeutic cream over an aggravated shoulder. "What's wrong fellas? Too much cheese? Need more? Are you worried if you order too much cheese for your pasta that you won't be able to eat through it? Don't worry, it'll melt. So do we have a deal?"

At the request of Robert Towell, the waitress returned with a giant plastic cheese grater that, according to Towell's recollection, had a harness on it. "This was the turning point of the deal, I wasn't going to leave until all the cheese in the restaurant had been grated, and the deal was done,"

Towell wrote in his infamous unpublished memoir.

For all parties, the afternoon felt good and relaxed. When the parmesan cheese crank came with the waitress, Towell just kept on nodding until a beard of cheese lay over his plate.

"Sir, I have run out of cheese," the waitress said.

"Yes, you have. We'll be in touch," Robert Towell said, and dismissed her.

Towell could no longer see the meal, the men or the restaurant; he was filtered through a system of pre-arranged product placement. It brought tears to his eyes. *The fifth frame is brought to you by Jim's Hardware, home of the 20-cent lug nut, right in the heart of Niagara Falls on Maple Drive.*

A match made in entrepreneurial heaven, Robert Towell thought, and he would play the part of corporate friendly Bob.

"I think we can sponsor you, for awhile, you seem to know what you are doing."

"Fellas, this will take off, it already has. I can send you more of our surveys. Understand this, my research proves people are tired of the way bowling is presented on television. And I'm not about to suggest that I throw a couple of bimbos with nice tits into the lanes and call it bowling, no. We want families to enjoy the programming as well. Notice how no child has ever clamoured to own bowling sports action figures, or demanded bowling posters on their walls? That's going to change. I'm not about to alienate half my market by pissing off parents nation-wide."

"He's got a point Charlie," one of the red-faced men said, tearing into a piece of heavily buttered bread.

"So we're good?"

"You have a deal," the businessmen said in disturbing unison.

Only after the lunch was over and the locals had left did Towell turn to Lebelle and smile. "You did good, thanks."

Later, in private, Towell offered Lebelle valuable insight into the plans for the company. "I'm the bad guy right now in bowling, because I want to change it. We are going to have to find a new audience. Bowlers, most of them, will hate us. I hope you're ready."

The men slept in their separate beds in the double room, their battery-filled smoke detectors beeping through their sleep. This sense of fuzzy security was warmly woven through the unwritten first script which would later become the first-ever WCB pay-per-view.

WCB PROMOTIONAL VIGNETTE:
(ROBERT TOWELL/ WCB SCRATCH VIDEO)

Production note: A simple shot of Robert Towell in a bowling alley explaining the game to the camera. There are two actors taking turns bowling. They are normal in every way. However, as Towell's speech continues, the scratch inserts begin to flicker into the edit. Every ten seconds a black and white "scratch insert" (indicated in script by "X") begins to flick into the otherwise normal video. The "scratch inserts" vary: from a raging WCB bowler in mid-brawl, a pin across someone's jaw, a fist wrapped in chain, punching an opponent who is trying to throw a bowling ball while on his stomach. Robert Towell presents himself with sincerity, clean, but with a subtle contempt for the bowling society.

V/O: *The following announcement has been paid for by*
World Championship Bowling.

ROBERT TOWELL:

In bowling, the players take turns. The first bowler rolls his first ball, then waits patiently for the automatic pinsetter to reset the remaining pins. As the pinsetter does its job, ("X") an automatic ball returner grabs the ball, puts it on a conveyer belt, and returns it to the approach area. The first bowler rolls his second ball. The bowler takes his third ball. ("X") This time the automatic pinsetter knocks down any pins that are still standing and sets down a fresh rack of pins for the second bowler. ("X") Sound familiar? I'm sure it does. Look, it's up to you. The bowling alleys are there for you to use. But what if one element was added? ("X") What if skill wasn't enough? What if charisma suddenly mattered? How about machismo? Aggression? Terror? ("X") What if fear mattered? Come rise now, you the pathetic consumer. I'm just kidding. You are not *all* pathetic. ("X") Let us draw crowds, blood, and put bowling, as you know it, out of its impotent and geriatric misery. ("X") I'm Robert Towell, owner of World Championship Bowling. It's simple. Just pick a side.

V/O: *The preceding announcement has been paid for by*
World Championship Bowling.

THORNCLIFFE BOWLERAMA
EAST YORK, ONTARIO
DECEMBER 19, 1996

STRIKE: All ten pins down on the first ball. See also: double, turkey, four- and five-bagger, and six-pack. Seven, eight, nine, ten and eleven strikes in a row are called seven-in-a-row, eight-in-a-row, etc.

STRIKE OUT: To get all three available strikes in the tenth frame or, similarly, finish the game from any point with strikes.

STROKE: The arm and hand motion during the act of delivery over the foul line.

SWEEPER: 1) A wide-breaking hook which carries a strike as though the pins were pushed with a broom; **2)** a night of league bowling, previously designated, where bowling fees go toward high-scoring individuals or teams for that night.

ROBERT TOWELL had been approached about a bowling comeback on the set of *Pumpkin Seeds* in 1990, but refused to discuss his sporting past and threatened to fire his agent on the spot. "I felt betrayed, and I was marinating in this constant state of pain and anxiety over the decision I had made about bowling. My parents loved me in that sport, but they never just plain loved me alone, only in the context that I was a winner. That I was special so long as I was a bowling champion. I just wanted to be a kid. No lesson was ever learned from my bowling years but contempt and disgust for passivity. I looked at the stands and saw the parents watching us and felt like I was a part of a child pornography ring, and I was the best. There was no comfort in being the best. It was like being a smallpox champion. I hated those spectators. I thought, get a fucking life and quit staring at me. Let me grow up naturally."

The embryonic stages were over, the corpses were now scattered, newborn eyes saw the shape, the edge of the beast. This was Towell's vision, and everyone around the new company felt the eerie buzz.

There was about twenty minutes before the force-fed crowd would fill the alley, thanks to complimentary tickets, radio give-aways and other acts of desperation. Robert Towell was pacing in the makeshift office, somewhere between the maintenance room and the snack bar supply closet. He was on a phone, leaving a message for a journalist who was profiling WCB in an upcoming magazine spread. Of course the notion of this attention made Towell simultaneously greedy and self-conscious. "Hello? All right, Gina, this is a message for Gina McSherry. I suppose, to answer your question, which has just now reached me, I wanted to do something that had never been done before but that was too easy. Everyone does that. I wanted it to reflect my actual mental state, my actual desire for a better tomorrow. Right now, as I leave this message for you, I want you to know that it could have been different. There is no other way for me to see this sport anymore but as an underground tumour. About a year ago, I was on a bus, half-asleep, traveling back from my ill-fated internship at Brunswick in Ohio, when I had this state-of-the-art dream. I was this old wrinkled man and I was on a ladder. I was looking up, so I had no idea where I was, nor did it seem important to me to know where I was at the time. It was bright and my hands trembled. I was holding an expired light bulb in one hand, while screwing in the new one, trying to balance on the ladder. Suddenly, a shudder charged through my body, like a current, but it wasn't from the light bulb. I was now falling, and it was only as I fell that I realized I was in the middle of a bowling lane. I hit the ground with the ladder, still not sure what had pushed me over, still feeling this immense shudder of power in the room. The impact broke parts of my body, mainly my ribs, but more importantly, Gina, my fall had cracked open the skin of the lane, and there was this pink and grey lava foaming and bubbling. I awoke, and like some medieval pneumonia, the dream and its meaning grew, fungus-like throughout my consciousness. Was I the old man? Was I the ladder? Was I grey lava? I'll let you interpret the dream as you like, and I expect to see you at our first pay-per-view BOWLFEST, this Sunday. Jerry likely has sent you some complimentary passes, and perhaps even some of our practice footage from rehearsals. All the best, thanks again for your patience."

He stormed out of his temporary office and with asteroid speed, took a walk around the alley, watching the minions at work with gaff tape and cord, with boom mics and white balance.

"Listen, Jerry? Yeah, good. I know it sounds weird back in the truck but it sounds fine here." Towell continued multi-tasking with walkie-talkies, payphones, and the bowling alley PA; whatever it took.

Meanwhile, sitting on top of a pile of the brand new NIK catalogue, Nikola was relaxing in the office with Katherine Cockshutt, preparing the spring line-up of accessories and nearly invisible thong-like hand warmers for winter club-goers.

"These photos of Martina are lovely Katherine," Nikola said.

Martina Sorbara as photographed by Katherine Cockshutt for the 1997 NIK catalogue.

"Thanks," Katherine acknowledged.

"Hold on," Nikola said, motioning to her desk. "It's my line."

Robert paced with the phone in one hand and a walkie-talkie in the other, eyes jotting all over the building.

"Nikola, it's Robert. Robert Towell."

"I know who it is. You don't have to be so formal."

"Nevertheless, we're going to air in about three minutes. How are things at headquarters?"

"I'm upstairs, but I just double-checked everything in your office, you're fine."

"Good, so no last minute changes?"

"No."

"And how is your work going? You get the catalogue done?"

"Yes, we're on schedule. The girls are just napping. Soon we're going to have a pillow fight and make out."

"That all sounds highly doubtful, but it sounds good," he said, watching two crew members hang the WCB banner over lane fifteen. "No, sixteen! Listen, I have to go to the truck and make sure the VTR operator knows his cues for the slow-motion replays, and I have to round up some audience."

"Audience?"

"I sent Dragan out about an hour ago to the food courts to get some people to come to this, so when we show it and try and sell it around it looks like there's a healthy audience."

"The food court, oh, how sweet."

"How much longer are you working at the office?"

"I don't know, not much longer, I don't think the girls can wait much longer, they keep paging me. I'm buzzing right now."

"Okay, well I guess I'll call you later."

"Robbie, you're being nice to everyone, right? Calling them by their names and not just, Hey you?"

"Yes. For the most part. Unless I don't like them."

"For example, Dragan's friend his name is, let's see, Dale, Dale Godfrey. It's right here in the WCB employee directory," Nikola said, the earnestness in her voice clearing forests and burying ruins. She was like sun block in the morning, protective and sweet.

"Yes, I'm sure I'll learn all their names once I go over the script again. I'm doing play-by-play anyway, so I'll have to refer to them at some point tonight."

"I'm just trying to show you how to be nice."

"Thanks, I really wouldn't know where to start. But I must go now."

"Take care. Talk to you later. And good luck."

Robert Towell hung up. He approached the lip of the counter, and waited until the manager was paying enough attention before he began the insults. "You guys seem really unclean down here," he told the manager with disdain. "I'll be back, we're just making sure the feed works."

The manager said nothing, and returned to his disinfection duties at the shoe swamp. Out in the parking lot Robert Towell scanned the sea of cars for the WCB van.

"It's all set boss."

"Now I want this done right, just cause we're not live tonight doesn't mean we can afford mistakes. I want it perfect from take one," Towell said to the group of technicians in the belly of the van.

"Boss, I have the replay loop of Greg Lebelle in training as well as Dragan Momchilo stretching. Now you want us to couple those images with those of the fat overweight and bald bowlers that we shot earlier today?"

"Yes, think if you will of good and evil, night and day. Bowling as it was before now, and bowling as it will be ten minutes from now. I'll leave the rest up to you. You have the material to portray things in a manner of which I will approve. If you don't, I'll hire someone else to edit it. It's up to you. The job is yours. Remember, this is likely the only time we won't be live. So let's do things just the same as if we were live. Okay boys?"

"Okay boss," the VTR operator said. "It'll be fine."

"Good," Robert Towell nodded and left the van, heading back down into the throat of the bowling alley stairway which culminated at the overweight doors that would open, releasing his brand of bowlers to commence World Championship Bowling's first-ever pay-per-view: BOWLFEST.

The cars began to fill the small parking lot; some were just there to shop at the Zellers, while others, the braver ones, were there for the show.

Inside the stew of the complex, camera operators were positioning themselves sniper-like amongst the fountain pop dispensers. One such tech-jockey fashioned a rope and raised himself up along a set of pipes just south of lane sixteen to secure a camera for an aerial view. The crew had to be inventive to combat the awkward and primitive structure. Yes, these fixtures, pipes, logos and lockers on which Towell's crew affixed themselves seemed entirely fossilized. "Who designs these places? The mentally ill?"

"How's it going?" one crew member said to the other.

"This Towell guy is a bit out there, so don't talk back to him; whatever he says, whatever you think he wants to hear, just say as little as possible."

"Why?"

"Trust me."

An aerial camera was rigged right above lane sixteen. This camera would be used in post-production cutaways, replays of key "turn-overs".

Robert Towell approached the inner crew, handing them napkins.

"I'm ordering us some really greasy food when this thing is over."

"Okay, sounds great," one of them said.

"Let's make this place seem uglier than it actually is. Let's really get the aesthetic into the consciousness, so we can stand to profit by its reconstruction," he explained to his crew. He was now pacing and grinning. He rattled his knuckle on the manager's counter until someone noticed.

When the manager's attention seemed permanent, Towell began his gruesome crusade.

"Do you have any ugly people working in the back?"

"What kind of event are you having here?" the manager asked, looking at the WCB logo swivel into position above lane sixteen.

"I'm not paying you to ask questions," Robert Towell hissed.

"I understand sir, it's just that I don't want to blow a fuse or anything with your…"

"I'm paying you for lane sixteen and your environmental co-operation. More money than you'd make from ten fatties and their sisters, so just relax and put things into historical perspective."

The manager recoiled without words.

"Stupid cog," Towell muttered.

For the regulars it was just another night off, as Towell surmised in the pages of his unpublished memoir, *The Man Who Murdered Bowling*: "For the regulars, it was just another suburban night of fatalistic decay, but for WCB, this was a dress rehearsal for the great living death, a painful spin-off no one wanted to be cast in. This particular bowling alley, if not every last one, was pungent with the ground-in scent of dead lung tar. Puke patterned carpeting came into focus, the dolly shot moved from the doorway, zooming out and widening."

From his jacket pocket Towell pulled out a pair of vintage goggles from the Gulf War and began to encircle the crew as he barked orders.

"Camera two," Towell yelled into the walkie-talkie. The WCB logo was lowered from the ceiling while a small amount of pyrotechnics licked the edges of the letters. The house lights went out completely.

"Adjust the colour balance there please," Towell ordered.

After a few confused moments with some maladjusted vending machines and an unemployed real estate agent from Leaside, he found the manager again, who looked as if tears were building up in his eyes.

"You fucking idiot, you blew my fuse," the manager shouted.

"Would you chill out?" Towell replied rather harshly. "Idiot? You're the one who works *here*."

Robert Towell multi-tasked as he watched the manager fix the fuse. From a yellow case he took out his wireless microphone and attached it to his belt. He then took out a second case from his jacket pocket which held a stick microphone with a WCB logo.

The manager restored the power and shook his head in disgust. But he couldn't really complain, WCB had paid him well, and in advance. Plus, Towell had signed a waiver, saying the company would be responsible for any damage. Jerry Tomlin even had a lawyer check out the paperwork.

"Okay boys in the truck, can you hear me? Let's test the sound level, and the spotlight on lane sixteen. Hit the lights." Towell walked into the middle of the lane and turned the microphone off. Giving the finger to the manager, Towell yelled back: "This is what I'm paying you for?" The manager shrugged in disgust. A mild anger began to build up until his hand ran across the wad of money Robert had lodged in his pants earlier in the evening. "And you can keep the fucking birthday cake, asshole. We aren't here for any formal celebration."

According to witnesses Robert Towell did end up taking the complimentary birthday cake home afterwards, but he denies it.

In the truck the crew prepped a thirty second trailer for the new WCB superstar "Hollywood" Dragan Momchilo. It was nothing fancy, a few wipe edits, a few jarring fonts, the central theme was "arrival". Clips of the young man stretching in a gym, playing soccer, pacing in front of a fresh set of pins, and riding in Dale Godfrey's pick-up.

"He doesn't look very tough," the VTR operator said.

"No, the boss says he's barely eighteen, plays a lot of soccer. I saw him talking to himself at a grocery store one night."

Next, the crew played a similar segment of new WCB superstar Greg "Agamemnon" Lebelle eating boiled potatoes, carrying a tree trunk in the woods, eating a plate of tacos, smoking, and finally, tackling three stereotypical bowlers to the ground, crushing one of their glasses, and mussing all of their hairdos. The crew were frightened.

"Is this him training?"

"I guess so."

"He looks like a Viking. I love that man," Towell beamed on his walkie-talkie, watching the playback from the WCB desk.

It was nearing show time. Robert Towell stood under the WCB logo while a cameraman framed him. *Robert Towell, WCB owner.* Red light.

"Ladies and Gentlemen, Welcome to BOWLFEST!" Most of the patrons of the Thorncliffe Bowlerama barely looked up from their sodas, heavy carbohydrates and thick malt cocktails. Their guts hung over their belts. For the most part they were totally unaffected.

"Tonight in lane sixteen, we will see my new bowling organization take over professional and recreational bowling. And it won't be that hard either. I am now challenging anyone, any league player, any idiot beer-bellied bastard in the vicinity to get a partner and compete, in a friendly game against my two top players, Greg 'Agamemnon' Lebelle and 'Hollywood' Dragan Momchilo."

Backstage, with less than two minutes before the pandemonium was released, before the polyester wave began its slow locust chomp "Hollywood" Dragan Momchilo, the new face in WCB with a newly signed twenty year contact, smoked nervously. Beside him, standing five and a half feet tall was Dale Godfrey.

Lane sixteen at Thorncliffe Bowlerama.

"So you're the special referee?" Momchilo asked.

"That's what Rob told me," said Godfrey pointing to Jerry Tomlin who was pacing with a microphone and casing the backstage area while a floor director waited patiently for her chance to pick his brain.

"I think we should shoot it here," Tomlin said with intensity.

"Okay, I'll grab the guys," the floor director said, feeling the nervous energy that was starting to spread throughout the crew and talent.

Momchilo was puzzled, Godfrey had only part of the puzzle.

Both men took lasting drags from their cigarettes, knowing they'd have to slow down for the upcoming match. Momchilo pumped Godfrey for more details.

"So what is supposed to happen?"

"I don't know. You bowl, and they haven't told me anything more than that."

"But who am I fighting?" Momchilo asked.

"You and some big guy are a team. They've got no opponents for you yet. They're getting them from the crowd or something." Godfrey shrugged and walked down the hallway, through the curtain and out into the spectacle Towell had whipped up.

Jerry Tomlin swung by and nodded to the young Serbian.

On cue and with a modest amount of pomp and indoor pyrotechnics, "Hollywood" Dragan Momchilo walked through the backstage door into a flood of activity. The moment the curtain was touched World

Championship Bowling would commence. As he moved his tiny frame down the hall, Momchilo's eyes nearly exploded into tears as the shadow grew flesh, and his first-ever glimpse of the behemoth grin of Greg Lebelle came into view, swallowing the landscape.

"Hey man, you look exactly like your picture," the large-framed clean shaved man said with a bull-glaring face.

"What picture?" Momchilo retorted, a bit choked up with fear.

"I'm Greg, let's do this man."

"Okay, what are we suppose to do?"

"Trust me, just follow my lead."

Jerry Tomlin dashed up to the men before they entered the alley. "Here," Tomlin said, stiffly handing Momchilo a pair of handcuffs. "Lebelle will cue you." Greg Lebelle winked at his new sidekick as they walked through the curtain.

By this time Towell had lured two league professionals to lane sixteen. The match began as a traditional bowling contest. The first frame began clumsily enough, with both teams matching each other's spares after some heckles from the crowd. Towell grew impatient. He signalled for Lebelle to move the game into its new physical and aggressive host. He took a swig of gingerale to foster his bad mood.

"Yeah, strike," said the league pro to his partner. It was a nice shot, clean, crisp, with a short air time, the release was textbook. Suddenly, the celebration was deflated into an adrenaline rush parachuted out of nowhere.

"What the fuck are you doing?" the league pro said, as Greg "Agamemnon" Lebelle hoisted him up by the throat and slammed his lower back onto the ball return. He placed the pro's leg across it.

"Lebelle is working on that leg," Tomlin said.

Lebelle grabbed a fan's folding chair and smashed it over the vulnerable kneecap. The bowler clamped his knee in shocked pain.

"I don't think he saw that coming," Towell said to Tomlin.

The hoodwinking continued, and with the score of team WCB (Momchilo and Lebelle) 10 points behind the league locals, Robert Towell cued more chaos. This time, Lebelle tossed Dragan Momchilo a set of handcuffs and yelled, "The guy in the yellow shirt, to the railing over there!" In an instant that contained all of the youth's sportsmanship integrity and childhood Popsicle innocence, Momchilo, wearing a hand-cut blue T-shirt and track pants, sweat bands with matching headband, grabbed his yellow-shirted opponent and knuckled him in the jaw with the edge of the steel cuffs.

"Aw, fuck whataya doing man?" the hapless bowler protested, only to be kicked in the side of the face, tangled in the unexpected violence, knuckles, claws, fisted rounds to the breadbasket. It was this combination of strangling and stomach bruising that allowed the Serbian youth to handcuff his opponent to the iron rail that outlined the snack bar eating area. As Momchilo cuffed him to the rail he apologized even as he pummeled the older athlete. "Sorry," Momchilo said.

"Don't say sorry!" Towell fired.

"Why?" Momchilo replied to the announcer's table.

"Are you a Carebear?"

"No."

"And don't call anyone your friend, we'll have to edit it out," Towell said with pre-arranged hostility.

Momchilo turned to the cuffed bowler and did his job. The bowler's hands tried to protect his own throat but Momchilo broke through the block and kicked him in the stomach. Then, as if a fleet of scientists were monitoring and manipulating him from a nearby laboratory, upping the voltage ever so slightly, Momchilo took some of the cable feed into his hands and began to strangle the yellow-shirted bowler.

Tomlin cried: "Business has just picked up here at BOWLFEST, Momchilo is teaching this pro what it means to play ball here in WCB!"

Meanwhile, the WCB team's anchor Lebelle hoisted the other league local up in his arms and threw him halfway down the lane.

"That's gotta be frustrating for this local pro," Tomlin surmised.

Confused and embarrassed, the bowler got to his knees in an effort to recover, but Lebelle began to charge him, bull-like, tackling him squarely against the well-buffed wood.

"At least you're with the grain," Lebelle snorted to the confused man. Lebelle grabbed some cable feed and wrapped his opponent's feet together and began dragging him towards the announcer's table.

The ball run chortled with movement. To Towell, it was a heavy drug pumping through the building's veins in heavy doses. "I have no idea what Greg Lebelle has planned for this poor soul, but it's not going to be pretty," Robert Towell exclaimed to the crowd and to the viewers at home.

Trying to turn over onto his stomach, dizzy and sore, the pro crawled in the opposite direction, towards the pins, against the wave of Lebelle's pull. Lebelle stopped pulling him and signalled for Momchilo to join in his fight. The duo began throwing balls into the tangled bowler's legs, arms and back until he eventually rolled into the gutter of the next lane.

Lebelle and Momchilo knocked down the remaining pins, taking time to peek behind the mechanics of the pinsetter.

"What's back there? I've always wanted to know," Momchilo asked.

It was their opponent's turn to bowl, but both, thanks to World Championship Bowling's new brand of rules, were incapacitated. It was then that Robert Towell proudly injected a new rule for professional bowling: *An incapacitated bowler who can't throw when it is his turn will get a score of zero for that frame, thanks to some well placed gutter balls by the surviving members of competition.*

As he read the rule aloud at the WCB announcer's table, the words appeared onscreen. This is biblical, Towell thought, snorting proudly. His mind felt large as the cameras soaped up the rest of the action.

As Lebelle and Momchilo towered over the fallen game, taking their position for the money shot that would appear on WCB.COM later that night, as the local league regulars who attempted to rescue their fallen war veterans were carted off, the intention of the work was evident: Robert Towell's new redemption clause in pro bowling's fate had just been implemented with precision.

The new *it* duo of 5-pin bowling snarled into the cameras, arms raised with tattooed bravado. Robert closed the segment with an address to the sporting world. From the desk with Jerry Tomlin by his side, a very proud Robert Towell summed up the evening with great enthusiasm: "The new pugilistic movement in professional bowling has arrived. Looks like our winners tonight are Greg 'Agamemnon' Lebelle and 'Hollywood' Dragan Momchilo, thanks for tuning in, this is World Championship Bowling, and we'll see you next time."

The cameras shut down, went limp. Momchilo stood next to his handcuffed opponent, shaking his head amidst the chaos.

"What an opener," Tomlin congratulated Towell. "Did you expect that sort of buzz? This crowd is livid."

"It's good news, that's all I can say. I can't think right now for some reason."

The handcuffed league pro was hissing at the crew. As Lebelle and Momchilo walked by, he exploded, "What the fuck was that all about?"

"Just doing his job," Lebelle backed him up. "Let's go, we're due at the club soon."

"Get me out of these cuffs," the loser cried.

"What club?" Momchilo asked.

"I'm taking you out, we're going to be best friends," Greg Lebelle said.

On his way out of the stagnant alley, up the gum-daubed stairwell, out into the open parking lot air, Robert Towell nodded to the bowling alley manager, signalling he'd be with him in a moment.

Jerry Tomlin joined the men. Towell signed a form and handed it back to Tomlin's loyal hand.

"Talk to ya tomorrow boss," Tomlin said, and walked towards his car. "Not too early."

Towell turned to the manager and frowned, "Thanks for your environmental co-operation." The manager's only reaction was to look down at his bowling hand to double-check that all his fingers were there.

BALLS & BRAWL: WCB & THE NEW BOWLING AS S&M MORALITY

by Gina McSherry

I watched from the stands with three of my girlfriends. The men were designed to inspire, but it was their vulnerability that drew us in. It was the unspoken, the unmoving moments that caught our attention. It was in those quick milliseconds in between prearranged gutters and rental shoe slapstick, when one of the men would lean into his opponent asking, "Are you okay?" In those candid exchanges comfort was provided for all of us, though most of the fans surrounding us just wanted a result. The ideology of the female WCB fan goes beyond the blood and guts that Towell wants to provide us. It goes beyond the lunch pail, it's the live aromatics, anticipating those lovely flaws in production that provide the real human experience, that is the fetish, the innate voyeurism connecting all of us. For my own pleasure, violence is secondary, the pain is secondary. It's the comfort and the aftercare that leaves a permanent scar, one to treasure. Violence is simple; we have it in our films, in our news, in our other sports. What is the real storyline here? Towell is concluding perhaps that men have outgrown the social and spatial limitations of bowling. So many questions early on in the match, and I've only just started my foot-long hot dog.

— From *Xtreme Sports & Mind Almanac (Winter, 1996)*

THE RULES

(WORLD CHAMPIONSHIP BOWLING)

EACH WCB MATCH SHALL BE NO LONGER THAN FIVE FRAMES. THE WINNER SHALL BE DECIDED BY THE APPOINTED REFEREE, BUT MORE OFTEN THAN NOT, THE HIGHEST SCORE WINS. IF YOUR OPPONENT CANNOT FINISH A FRAME DUE TO INCAPACITATION, DON'T JUST STAND THERE, RUSH THE GUTTER! IT IS PERFECTLY LEGAL TO ROLL GUTTERS FOR HIM DURING HIS ABSENCE.

STANDARD

The first frame is an unmitigated exchange, a normal bowling match (as close as is possible). The final four frames are full contact, hand to hand combat, with partial use of weapons allowed (at referee's discretion) such as hammers, bats, chains, and brass knuckles. The preliminary round of BOWLBRAWL for example, in which Greg "Agamemnon" Lebelle used the popcorn tank on his opponent, was an automatic disqualification.

NO DISQUALIFICATION

Full contact match from the opening frame. In this type of match, usually at the top of a pay-per-view card or even a championship match, one competitor waits for his opponent at the foul line. His opponent rushes him from the back, they fight, and try to prevent each other from scoring. The frames go by fast, because of all the gutters and interference. This is a defensive game as much as it is offensive. There are also usually numerous bowlers "running in" to swerve the score by rolling gutters. The locker room can be a place to persuade fellow bowlers to become allies, or plot against a top dog. This is usually a fast match, with the score and skill taking a back seat to hand to hand combat.

HARDCORE

Usually reserved to settle an unresolved score, these matches are drawn up in blood, the contracts are signed and the outcome is decided by who is left standing. The feud has to be sold. Lebelle and Momchilo's feud was vastly tracked on the Internet and through a few filmed vignettes that sold the storyline. However, there were still some remnants of tradition involved. To be considered a "bowling" match, there has to be at least one bowling "transaction". In the case of an enclosure match (such as WCB DEVASTATION) each bowler had to record a single pinfall before qualifying to escape the "structure". The winner was the first bowler to knock down a single pin and leave the "structure". There are also handcuff matches (WCB BOWLFEST), inferno matches (WCB INVASION), and impromptu chainsaw matches (WCB BOWLBRAWL).

ROBERT & NIKOLA'S APARTMENT

TORONTO, ONTARIO
DECEMBER 19, 1996

With a valid driver's license in his wallet nudging an erotic photobooth picture of Nikola and a rubber snake, Robert Towell pulled into his underground parking lot. He took a package of licorice off the dashboard, shut the driver's side door and clicked his car alarm. It made a robotic noise which always made Robert smile. Soon there would be the sex.

Inside their apartment, Nikola waited, naked, mouth full of licorice. Robert Towell chased her; she stopped at a table for a container of whipped cream and began to spray him.

"You didn't shake it enough."

"You shake it," Nikola instructed. "Shake it Robbie," she repeated.

The bathtub was filled with foamy lather.

"Was it a good night?" Nikola asked.

"Yes, oh yes," he replied, opening the fresh licorice, watching her like a piece of fresh prey. "And you? How are weekend retreat bookings going? Are the sponsors obeying you? How are your designs coming for the new season Mrs. Towell?"

"Good, now fuck me you brute," she cackled.

After that nonsense was over, they packed up the car for the holidays. Robert wore his hooded winter coat and fluorescent green toque.

In the morning there would be no time to pack, shopping would eat up all of their day. Nikola was making back-up gravy for the Christmas dinner and Robert was wrapping the gifts for all the cousins he had never met.

Nikola did her make-up and changed the answering machine message as the afternoon dipped into evening. "Nice toque Robbie."

"I told you that I cannot see black cotton. I have told you on more than one occasion that I need a bright colour, the last thing I want is to be caught in a rush in the winter and having to scramble in a room carpeted in black socks, underwear and sweaters and not being able to find my toque. That is a huge fear for me."

"Well, you're a brave man," Nikola smirked. "Now take my bag down to the car."

"I just took a bag. How much shit do you need to bring?"

"I'm bringing *you* aren't I? Those are gifts in there, so don't worry, it's a one-way hassle."

"Thank the Maker. Now, I figure if we leave in the next ten minutes we'll be at your Mom's by 6:00 PM, giving us time to take a shower and then eat."

"A shower?"

"Yes. I'm not smelling of new car and recycled breath."

"You're insane. We're not walking into my Mom's place and saying Merry Christmas, where are your towels we need to shower now."

"Why not?"

"Because it's Christmas, not a television appearance. We are there to see the family. Not wash. Shower now."

"I already did. I'm just saying, what if there is a lot of air pollution and it comes in through the filter, and we start to spoil?"

"Okay, I'm ready, turn off those lights."

"IT WAS PERHAPS NOT OBVIOUS, BUT TRUTH BE TOLD, I HAD NO FAITH IN THE PEOPLE I CHOSE TO PROMOTE. MY MANTRA WAS UNCONDITIONAL, I WOULD PROVIDE THE ANTIDOTE FOR BOWLING, AND I DIDN'T CARE WHO WAS THERE HOLDING THE BALLS. THAT WAS SOMETHING SPECIAL THAT JUST OCCURRED NATURALLY, THE WAY THE PLAYERS INTERACTED, THE WAY THE ROSTER FILLED OUT. I WOULD GET THE TAPES SHOWN ON LOCAL COMMUNITY BASIC ACCESS CHANNELS, AND IT GREW FROM THERE. SOMETIMES THE NINJA CHARACTERS WERE FEMALE RUGBY PLAYERS, OR ONCE I THINK IT WAS A TENNIS PLAYER. I BOUGHT A BOWLING ALLEY AT AN AUCTION THAT I ENDED UP BURNING DURING A TAPING FOR ONE OF OUR ONLY U.S. PAY-PER-VIEWS. FOR BRIEF TV SPOTS BLUE SCREENS BECAME MY BEST FRIEND, AS I TOOK A GIANT SCALPEL TO THE WORLD OF BOWLING. AFTER OUR FIRST YEAR WE HAD OUR OWN REGULAR PAY-PER-VIEW DEALS, THROUGH A SERIES OF LUCRATIVE SPONSORSHIPS. BOWLING IS NOW THE ONLY SPORTS RELATED EXPOSURE FOR TOBACCO COMPANIES. SINCE SMOKING WAS NEVER BANNED RECREATIONALLY, AND SINCE BOWLING ALLEYS ARE UNDERGROUND AND NO ONE TRULY CARES WHAT GOES ON DOWN THERE, NO LESS THAN THREE MAJOR TOBACCO FIRMS STARTED SPONSORING OUR EVENTS, ON THE CONDITION THAT OUR BOWLERS WOULD TAKE THE OCCASIONAL PUFF ON CAMERA."

— Robert Towell in the March 1997 issue of *Modern Bowling*

GISELLA HOME

MISSISSAUGA, ONTARIO
DECEMBER 20, 1996

Robert Towell paced in front of the giant clay vat of gravy. Several large cats were etched in blue on the outside of the vat, and it was sitting on a separate table from everything else. Robert noticed that virtually every condiment had its own table.

"So Robert, Nikola says business is going well."

"Yes, she is telling you the truth," Robert replied.

"When are you two going to give me a granddaughter?"

"What kind of granddaughter do you want?" Robert replied.

"I'm sorry I don't follow you Robert," Nikola's mother said politely.

"I'll look into it, I can check the lost and found at headquarters on Monday."

ROBERT & NIKOLA'S APARTMENT

TORONTO, ONTARIO
EARLY DECEMBER 21, 1996

Robert Towell turned off the dark blue U2 bomber-shaped nightlight beside the bed and kissed Nikola's bare ass goodnight. Her nightstand, with fax machine and snow angel was dimming on a timer. He kissed her neck and then her ass again. It would be the last time he saw either part for nine hours, or so he thought. When they awoke in the middle of the night they made sloppy love, sloppy because the sheets untucked themselves and Robert had this thing about stapling the sheets under the mattress, something he called "the real tuck" which he did every night before attempting sleep.

The phone rang at one-thirty. It was Nikola's mother.

"I just like it that way," Robert told Nikola's mother. He handed the phone to Nikola.

"Sorry Mom, it's just the way he likes it, he wanted to tuck in the sheets and it's a two hour drive. When his mind is set on something..."

"But you didn't even open your gifts," Nikola's mother replied over the phone.

"I'm sorry, I'm really sorry Mom, maybe next year."

WCB NEWSBOARD 1997-99

Former WCB investor and video game company Akklaim has filed for bankruptcy and shut its doors. Akklaim was working on several prototypes for WCB video game titles, most notably "BOWLBRAWL 2000" which boasted sixteen different types of matches, using a choice of 120 bowlers, including Black Ninja Six, Greg "Agamemnon" Lebelle, Jordan Binner and Dale Godfrey.

WCB head of talent Jerry Tomlin was seen at a soccer game on Tuesday. He stood alone and appeared to enjoy the game.

WCB has confirmed their next big event will be called "BOWLBRAWL" and an undisputed champion will be crowned. It is expected that this event will be the debut for both Dale Godfrey, Jordan Binner and two ninjas. A WCB spokesperson commented, "We are now going to establish our roster, not just our style of play."

Several concerned parent groups stationed themselves outside of WCB headquarters early last week to protest the excessive violence WCB is accused of promoting. "WCB is endorsing violence to a young and impressionable audience," says Jennifer Rainer, who organized the small rally. Rainer says WCB promotes violence at all levels of bowling, including recreational. "Towell is a former child bowling champion, for years he was seen as a role model. What he is doing is irresponsible. There have already been incidences of children getting in fights at school and at bowling birthday parties, trying to copycat WCB stars." While the company released no official statement, WCB spokesperson Jerry Tomlin assured the public that WCB had the best of intentions. "Our company is new, and when something is very new, it gets scrutinized, vilified.... I think movies, the news, music videos and other sports carry the same degree of violence, and everything we do should be taken with a grain of salt." Despite a few tempered incidences, no serious injuries have been reported.

WCB BOARD MEETING

TORONTO, ONTARIO
JANUARY 12, 1997

Jerry Tomlin and Robert Towell were walking dilingently down the hall in matching suits. They were, like the company, ready to ring in the modern bowling era.

"On its own I find this statistic shocking and disturbing, but combine it with the coincidental birth year of Greg Lebelle, wow. We're dealing with Satan himself on this passage into the sporting netherworld."

"What's the stat Rob?"

"Americans spent $43.6 million on bowling balls."

"In 1963?"

"Yup."

"Anything more current?"

"Why do you need to get more current than that, those are reasonable numbers. Those are great numbers."

Not everyone who sat on the WCB board knew the bare-bones story of Robert Towell's early bowling career. If they did they might have started feeling sinister, like being invited over to a friend's place for dinner only to discover you're the guest of honour at an assisted suicide party.

"All right everyone, let's get down to business," Robert Towell commanded, sitting down at the head of the table. Jerry Tomlin stood behind him, nodding at everyone present.

"Damn it. We need a champion. We need someone to be the franchise, the flagship," said one of the board members.

Nodding as he made himself comfortable in his chair, Robert Towell noticed his wife sitting beside him and thought playfully, *This is incredible. Everyone here is staring at my wife.* "So, how is everyone? Fabulous. This is it, the list of six bowlers who will compete in the first BOWLBRAWL tournament for the WCB undisputed championship in March," said Towell, and began to read the list:

JORDAN BINNER
DALE GODFREY
BLACK NINJA SIX
"HOLLYWOOD" DRAGAN MOMCHILO
GREG "AGAMEMNON" LEBELLE
BLACK NINJA SEVEN

One of the executives stood up, dusting a flock of cracker bits from his necktie and shirt.

"Rob, who is fighting who? Like what is the order?"

"I'm glad you asked Don, we want to keep Dragan and Greg apart until we have to pair them up in the tournament itself. I mean, it may happen in this tournament, or it may not, depending on who wins the first rounds, but I want to keep them apart until we have no choice but to use them together."

"Why is that?" another board member asked. For the moment Robert Towell was studying his wife's kneecaps, but realised a new voice was speaking. His name was Stanley and he was just married last year. He had moved up quickly, copy editing the first issue of *WCB Magazine,* designing parts of the WCB shopzone website, and doing some storyboards for cross-over commercial spots on local television.

Robert looked up from the kneecap. "Well Stanley, you see, until now it has seemed like Lebelle and Momchilo are pals. So we'll do it like this: 'Hollywood' Dragan Momchilo versus Black Ninja Six, Jordan versus Dale, Greg 'Agamemnon' Lebelle versus Black Ninja Seven."

"And then each of those winners of the first match will meet in the triple threat finale?" Stanley asked quizzically, trying to keep up, but mostly, trying to impress his boss.

"Exactly. You catch on quick," Robert smiled.

"I'm going to my 11:15 meeting," Nikola Towell, in wide lens Patricia Field sunglasses, announced to the room and pushed her chair back from the table. Robert watched his wife leave, in her yellow cigarette pants, then resumed with a sigh.

The meeting concluded with a script revision and orders for six WCB dolls that would hit stores in three weeks to promote BOWLBRAWL.

"These will retail for around ten dollars Canadian each," Towell said proudly, and began to sketch on his clipboard. "In fact, we should make a bowling alley play set, we could have two different ones, and maybe even make some announcers too, a bowling alley manager who the kids can have assaulted by Lebelle."

"Or one of the Ninjas."

"Yeah right." The room exploded in corporate cigar laughter.

"We could do one of your wife."

"Excuse me?"

"A doll of Nikola Towell."

"I don't think so. *I* don't even have a doll."

"I'm just joking boss."

"You're lucky I'm in a good mood, it's a long walk down to the first floor from that window, if you catch my drift."

After the meeting Robert Towell went upstairs but found Nikola Towell tied up in her meeting with *Nylon* magazine.

"She's been on the phone all afternoon," an assistant said.

"Tell her I miss her. I'll be back."

He returned to the WCB offices where Jerry Tomlin waited anxiously for Towell's signature for several orders, invoices and poster approval for mall appearances. "And there is also a fax for you from Clay Shallaghan. He's coming to BOWLBRAWL, says he wants to meet for lunch that day."

"That's fine, I can do a 3 o'clock lunch the day of at Hendersons or Velcro."

"So should we bring Momchilo and Lebelle in?"

"Yes, it would seem appropriate. Okay, gentlemen, if you want to take a bit of a break, we're going to talk to our talent now. Stay if you like, eat some food, let me know if you require anything okay?" Robert Towell signaled over to Jerry Tomlin. "Jerry, can you get the boys?"

With his light and manageable hair ever-parted, his slightly fat nose sniffing in the bright silence of the boardroom, his shirt and tie tight, tight enough to cause his face to redden, Jerry Tomlin filled up his glass with a cool offering of gingerale. He was sweating. He got up and found Momchilo and Lebelle smoking in the hallway and signalled for them to enter the boardroom.

"So, where did you come from again, work?" Greg Lebelle asked, noting his thin co-worker's extremely casual sweat-wear.

"Home. Just ate a big dinner," Dragan Momchilo said patting his flat stomach.

"Lucky bastard. I have to work after this. I'm starved," Lebelle said, looking around the room for a seat and some food.

"So? I have to work all day Sunday," Momchilo boasted. "Where are you working anyway?" Momchilo asked, changing the subject.

"I have a six week contract as a counsellor in training for this treatment centre, then they might hire me full time."

"What's this meeting about?"

"I don't know, talking merchandising I think, I want to see the new toys."

"And the shirts too."

"Yeah."

The second half of the meeting was full of laughter, the talent really brought out the best in everyone that afternoon. "We really were gelling," recalls Tomlin. Robert Towell read the script for a promo trailer aloud. This was followed by a merchandising report by Jerry Tomlin who announced the pending distribution of dolls and T-shirts.

"So, as you can imagine, we're quite excited about all this," Tomlin said, reaching for a stack of freshly printed colour catalogues. "Here is the catalogue if you gentlemen would care to have a look."

Greg Lebelle flipped through the glossy stapled leaflet quickly, hoping that his request for an AGAMEMNON T-shirt had not been cast aside. He wasn't disappointed. The shirt read *Greg* AGAMEMNON *Lebelle* on the front, and the back read *MISSILE-TOES*.

"I don't get it."

"Agamemnon? Wasn't he one of the twelve dwarfs?" Momchilo said with a creasy grimace that bordered on constipation.

"No, that was Sleazy," Robert Towell interjected. "Agamemnon was a Greek dentist who put his clients under, trimmed their pubic hairs and added the curly offerings to his sparse beard, then when they were of age, the sparse beards of his sons. They had this gene that made it nearly impossible to grow facial hair. Collectively they became the envy of many athletes in Greece, men and women, who literally would have killed for their facial hair, as this aided, and still does to my knowledge, in an athlete's speed."

"It's a majestic name Greg, we're happy for you to use it," Tomlin said with a proper smile. Robert nodded in agreement.

"Now, are we clear about the tournament? We're keeping you two separated for as long as we can, if you happen to wind up in the semifinals together, so be it, but we're hoping to keep you apart to draw interest in both your characters," Robert Towell said. "I think you both draw heat, you've both done well as of late."

"Yes, if I may interject," Jerry Tomlin began, "we're noticing both Dragan and Greg have tremendous numbers in entirely different age and gender demographics among our target audience. I'm not going to reveal any statistics, I mean this isn't a competition, but you guys are really a cut above everyone else in the locker room, and we really want to give you both pushes." Tomlin hesitated.

"In due time of course," Towell added.

"So who's going to win tomorrow?" Momchilo asked, chewing on a stir stick.

"Whoever survives the tournament, I mean we're not staging the ending. You will all be given the rules before you go in, it's up to you to decide what your course of action will be."

Robert Towell took a sip from his own personal stash of gingerale and chuckled for a moment, thinking of his coach. *Billy, I'm sure you're drowning in this rusty coloured fizz, somewhere in heaven, like a rotten-toothed goldfish thrashing on a patio deck, waiting for it to rain.*

He flipped through the catalogue and exhaled in no particular direction. "Jerry, we have to get these catalogues in tomorrow's newspapers, how hard will that be?"

"Very. I mean, I can get them into some, what about delivering them to cafés and malls and stuff like that, home deliveries?"

"Good thinking."

"All right, any questions gentlemen?"

"So who is in this tournament?"

"Your fellow WCB bowlers of course, you'll meet them next week at rehearsal. In fact, you met a couple of them last week. Those prospects, remember, from that luncheon we had with Ed Nervish? He's going to be selling some of our first line toys and we're pushing for the window display. Anyway, Jordan Binner, Dale Godfrey you know of course right, and a couple of Ninjas."

"Ninjas?" Lebelle said, looking at the catalogue with a bit more concern, finally catching a glimpse of a short man wrapped in black cotton pajamas and a mask holding a bowling ball.

Dragan Momchilo stared at Greg Lebelle, who returned the look. They were alone in the boardroom. Then they left.

"Why do you look so fucked up?" Lebelle asked.

"I don't know, just a bit wired, too much coffee," Momchilo replied.

"You look like you're, I don't know, you look like you're about to explode."

"I just had the weirdest weekend. Okay, check it out, I was at this girl's parents' cottage and they make me take care of their horses the whole time, like shoveling hay and stuff, building a fence, hey Dragan can you dig a moat for us? Then we go into town and this biker guy, all scrawny and tanned wearing this leather vest comes out, all drunk and says to me, *Snake Eyes? Is that you?* Then he goes on for about ten minutes with his buddies about how I saved his life in prison…"

"I don't want to hear any of this, it's so made up."

"No, I swear."

"Yeah, but the thing is, if these things really are happening to you, change your fucking life, cause no one wants to hear it."

Katherine Cockshutt: I never "loved" Black Ninja Seven, or Bruce, as his wife and kids knew him. It was purely physical — which suited me in the end more than it did him I think. It was pretty torrid at times, fucking in some bowling alley changing room or closet, his hands gripping my tits like it was the end of the world, licking my back and whispering, the sound of pins crashing just outside the door. I would blow him while he signed autographs. I could hear his voice, steady and calm, talking to fans like nothing was going on just under the table, like my mouth, everything wasn't full of him. I remember seeing his wife's shoes from under there once, right beside him, I imagined her arm resting on his shoulder, him smiling at her. I had tears streaming down my face, but I didn't stop, I didn't even blink. When he came I swallowed it. I lay on my back under the table looking at all the gum wads people had stuck there over the years and wished he would just come down and take me. I wanted to go public, fuck the PR, but he was so dedicated. He couldn't sacrifice his image, no matter how hard I made him. Shit really fell apart after the threesome with Black Ninja Seven and Six. I'd never done anything like that before, but I'm pretty sure Six had. He was balanced on one foot behind me pumping away and laughing and telling Seven how they had me stuffed at both ends with their swords. I just wanted him to shut up and fuck me, but I had Seven's cock in my mouth. Seven seemed uncomfortable, not jealous, just physically

uncomfortable. He was sitting on the sink, his hard cock just sticking out of his fly, staring at Six pump me, having the time of his life. In fact, they were both dressed, which struck me later as odd. I was the only one completely naked, they just had their cocks out, but totally clothed in their ninja outfits. I think they were even wearing shoes and socks. Seven kind of half-heartedly tried to grope me at one point, but Six's hands were everywhere, inside me and holding me, rubbing me. At one point Seven was fucking me as well, for a little while, but he could feel Six inside me — feel his own cock rubbing Six's. In the end Seven thought I was too good at taking on two men for someone who had never done it before. I sort of fell out of the WCB and got into curling after that.

Photo courtesy of WCB Archives.

WCB BOWLBRAWL

O'CONNOR BOWL
EAST YORK, ONTARIO
MARCH 9, 1997

SLOT GRIP: A grip on the bowling ball where the area between the third and fourth fingers is drilled away, resulting in one large finger hole.

SMALL BALL: Type of ball that doesn't mix the pins; must hit pocket perfectly for strikes.

SNAKE EYES: The 7-10 split. (bedposts, fence posts, goal posts, mule ears)

SNOW PLOW: A ball that clears all the pins for a strike.

SOFT ALLEY / SOFT LANE: A lane on which strikes come easy.

"WELCOME TO BOWLBRAWL!" The words exploded over the crowd. Some twirled fuzzy dice, some held large signs, and the rest were just a wash of cotton. Jerry Tomlin stood on a riser as the camera panned across the crowd, then dove at his face. "Hello folks, this is Jerry Tomlin, reporting live from the first-ever BOWLBRAWL where we will crown the undisputed WCB champion. I've just been sent word we are going live to Dale Godfrey's locker room where the contender is getting ready for his match. Apparently he's been given some disturbing news." When he spoke the sides of his mouth seemed to produce extra folds of skin.

In what became his traditional winter toque and miniature denim pants (29 inch waist, 27 inch leg) Dale Godfrey stood approximately five foot six inches, and had a coil of unkempt brown hair that was as close to an afro as could be fated. Despite his dwarfish representation, he was built up like a thoroughbred. His arm muscles were the size of most porn star waists, his neck was very large in proportion to the rest of him, and his pectoral region was all the firemen calendars bragged about and more. His tan was an emblem of his day job as a roofer.

Jerry Tomlin prepared for the interview. "We are moments away from the opening round of the tournament and now, inside the locker room of Dale Godfrey, we can see he has been told some upsetting news."

A few bowlers, including both Ninjas, scurried backstage, in and out of the shot.

"We don't know that for sure," Black Ninja Six said in the background filling up a paper cup with water. "He could be pretending. Most of this stuff never makes sense to me, there don't seem to be any rules."

Godfrey tore up phone books and overturned two garbage receptacles in his dressing room as Jerry Tomlin dashed to his side. "What is it Dale, Dale, please, let our viewers at home know what's bothering you."

Dale spat on the ground, pacing fanatically, his fists clenched, on edge; the microphone became a temporary exit for his pain. "I just found out, my girl, Judy, she's been sleeping with someone else. Some punk!"

"Do you have any idea who the perpetrator might be?"

"Someone with a cock."

"That doesn't narrow the field."

"It could be you. Did you make a deal with her?"

"No, Dale, please, I live with my mother and work for WCB almost twenty hours a day. When would I have the time?"

"All I know Jerry, all I fucking know is, I'm going to take out all my frustrations on whoever I'm fighting tonight."

"Perfect!" Jerry Tomlin replied, turning his gaze from Dale towards the camera. "Rob, that's all from here for now, take it away."

The camera panned over to Robert Towell, who sat with a headset at the WCB news desk, complete with two monitors, and replay access that sat directly in front of lane sixteen and the snack bar. "This is going to be something! A night like no other in the history of this business. Tonight a new champion will be crowned. The first match is between Black Ninja Seven and Greg 'Agamemnon' Lebelle. This should be interesting."

CLAY YOU ATTENDED THE INAUGURAL BOWLBRAWL PAY-PER-VIEW AND SAW BLACK NINJA SEVEN IN ONE OF HIS ONLY VICTORIES OVER GREG "AGAMEMNON" LEBELLE. WHAT DID YOU THINK OF THE NINJA OUTFIT?

Clay: A couple of things about the Ninja outfit: It's hard to see a guy dressed all in matte black walking towards his opponent in a dark bowling alley. [Towell] should have had some reflective tape or something. And Ninjas are not losers, that's why they wear black: because they are ruthless assassins and quite invincible. Black Ninja Seven is a mockery to the Ninja lifestyle and is probably symptomatic of Towell's thinly cloaked xenophobia.

Greg "Agamemnon" Lebelle walked in through the backstage area, past the snack bar, grabbing a bag of sour cream and bacon chips off the rack. The young snack bar cook looked up, youthful, determined, semi-numb from the toxins. He began to speak to the monster in a trembling moot protest. "Hey sir, you have to pay for that."

"No," Lebelle declared, his mouth stuffed with a knuckle full of chips. He relapsed back two paces for a napkin, his face still saying *No* to the boy and the world.

"Jerry, we are anticipating the debut of a new move from Greg 'Agamemnon' Lebelle tonight," Towell said from the broadcast desk.

"What's the new move?"

"All I know is that it's called missile-toes," Towell said smugly.

In his flimsy costume Black Ninja Seven quivered in front of the pins. His face was wrapped in black cotton, his black belt impotent. He rolled a spare after the first frame and Lebelle just laughed.

"Hey Towell," Lebelle roared with a smile shoplifted subconsciously from some Christmas morning memory, a childhood swindle. "Let me show you how we do it in the nineties! Watch this, boss."

And with that, Lebelle picked up the ball and threw it hard down the lane culminating in an excellent strike. Godzilla-like Lebelle picked up another and tossed it at Black Ninja Seven, catching him in the stomach. This was followed by a sucker punch to the hapless assassin's nose that sent him on his ass in front of the score desk. The ball Seven once held landed between his ankles and rolled into his groin. The crowd cheered and laughed, some booed, some wore Prada, some crushed piping hot morsels of fries against back molars, some swallowed their chewing gum.

Sensing a reaction from his opponent, Lebelle didn't let up, and ran towards the Ninja, who was getting his wind back. Lebelle put up one of his feet, pointing his toes like a ballet dancer.

"That connected right in the Ninja's guts, that's missile-toes, that's the move he promised to deliver tonight, and it looks like Seven is going to be the guinea pig," Tomlin screamed. Lebelle's pointed foot met Black Ninja Seven's jaw in an awesome crash. "Seven is not going to get up from that," Tomlin screamed. "It's all over. But wait, it appears as if Lebelle is going for another ball... he's motioning the cameras to follow him."

Robert Towell began to salivate as the events unfolded in the bowling alley, all live and recorded for the growing number of WCB subscribers. "Give them what they want Lebelle," Towell cheered from his seat lane side. "Folks, what's happening behind me is far more interesting than anything in televised bowling world-wide. This is WCB and this is Lebelle who is hungry! It appears that he's going back to the vending machine, he's going to bring it into play. This may constitute a disqualification as this is a preliminary match up in the tournament, and not the final in which of course, there are no rules."

Then, with flared nostrils, Lebelle pumped his arms and took a drag from his cigarette. He walked in big menacing horse clops towards the snack bar station and lifted up the giant popcorn tank.

"Oh my, Lebelle is on fire, and Black Ninja Seven wants no part of him."

"Strange strategy so early in the tournament, don't you think Jerry?"

"Well, these men know what's at stake, but can Seven even come back from the initial blow?"

Lebelle had the giant popcorn tank in his hands, the cord dragged behind him which unplugged somewhere along the psychotic journey.

"Insane!" Jerry Tomlin cried.

Lebelle began to cackle, wanting all to witness what he was bringing towards the lane.

Back at the desk Robert Towell jotted down notes for the extended VHS package he would release thirty days from the event and continued his verbal analysis, covering all the bases: "Black Ninja Seven doesn't know what to do," and this much was true. He pawed for a ball, rolled a gutter, followed by another gutter. "He has no strength," said Towell.

Seven's eyes were pre-occupied with the menacing image of Lebelle, who was coming closer. "Lebelle is serving Ninja pancakes tonight, it's not going to be pretty at all!" Tomlin screamed.

Dropping the popcorn tank on the Ninja's back, it took all of Lebelle's strength to keep it from killing him until WCB officials could put the machine upright. "That's it, I mean, there is only so much outside interference that the officials are going to allow, especially in a preliminary match," Towell said with disdain.

The WCB announcer: "Ladies and gentlemen the winner as a result of a technical disqualification, Black Ninja Seven." The grateful Black Ninja Seven shook his head in disbelief, crawled from his crumpled role under the appliance and headed backstage, exhausted.

The tournament continued and, as it did so, Robert Towell's joy blossomed. As each crippling bowling manoeuvre raced through the VTR in the truck and was broadcast live into the homes of dozens if not hundreds of pay-per-view subscribers, Towell's panacea was spreading.

"Folks, it looks like 'Hollywood' Dragan Momchilo will advance, he's got this one locked up." Momchilo turned to the camera and blew smoke into the screen and then towards Black Ninja Six.

"That's it, that was Six's last chance for redemption, all gutters, Momchilo wins it. Let's get the official word."

"Here is your winner, 'Hollywood' Dragan Momchilo!"

Backstage Greg "Agamemnon" Lebelle was in the shower, half of him was dry and smoking, taking a swig of Jack Daniels, the other lathered and working out a kink in his neck. Also backstage, Clay Shallaghan watched on a small monitor as "Hollywood" Dragan Momchilo loomed. He look confused. Upon turning the corner towards the showers, Momchilo ran into Jordan Binner, a youthful prospect who Towell had seen bowling in a local league and signed for peanuts.

"You seen Dale?" Momchilo asked.

"No, I'm facing him next though," Jordan said nervously.

"Fuck, he's pissed man, you better watch it, someone fucked his chick last night."

"Really? Yikes." Jordan's face was a silent wide mouth of static and soda, an expression that milked the moment, trying to think of something else to say. Trying but not that hard. "How was your match?" Jordan asked.

"Good. I beat the Ninja."

"Those Ninjas are such good guys to work with."

"Yeah, I know. Okay, I'm beat; fuck, I broke this guy's arm playing soccer last night, but it took something out of me on impact, and my back is killing me, I don't know if I can take any big pushes or bumps."

"That's too bad. Hope you can finish the tournament."

"Don't worry about that. I need to shower before the next match, so good luck with Dale. If I see him I'll try and calm him down."

"Thanks Dragan."

Back at the WCB broadcast desk, Robert Towell prepared the live crowd and the pay-per-view subscribed audience for the next match. "Folks, up next is another semi-final match up, Dale Godfrey against newcomer Jordan Binner. This should be interesting."

Jerry Tomlin added, "I've been watching Binner with a lot of interest at some of our house shows, and he's got a lot of intensity."

Robert Towell moved his attention to the tournament brackets that now appeared on the screen, with Dale Godfrey and Jordan Binner's name highlighted. "Jerry, what are your thoughts on this semi-final match?"

"All I know, the closer we get to the end of this thing, the more is at stake. This will determine who advances to the final for the undisputed WCB championship," Tomlin said with verve. "So we can only assume this match-up will be even more intense than previous rounds in the tournament."

To save production time, the introductions to some of the match-ups were done during commercial breaks, a tactic Towell had assured his sponsors would avoid any possible moments of "broadcast boredom" as he called it. As the event reconfigured itself from commercials into a clean dissolve to lane sixteen, Binner and Godfrey were already halfway through the first quarter of the game.

Robert Towell provided bleak interpretations of this match, which featured two bowlers he didn't particularly care for, but at least they were filling a gap in the roster.

"Folks, this match is not going to be pretty, neither man is particularly exceptional, or skilled, or clever, but they do possess one thing in common, and here she comes!"

Just then, as if cued, Godfrey's girlfriend Judy appeared by the snack bar carrying a plate of hot nachos.

"We seem to be in a tie here, and when there's a tie in World Championship Bowling, that means there are no rules. Next point wins!"

It was the ninth frame and both Binner and Godfrey had accumulated a laughable 102 points. Binner was up first and got 2 points. Godfrey needed three to advance in the tournament.

Backstage Momchilo watched, towel around his waist, tiny noodles of body hair dripping an eerie insecticide which glistened on his body. This was because he had recently seen a news report about suburban shower bugs who crawled out of showerheads.

"Come on Dale, two more points and we're in the finals together!" Momchilo shouted from the back.

As Godfrey lifted the ball for his final frame, he gauged the crowd. He looked at Binner who was pacing back and forth. From Binner's left emerged a familiar image. "Judy?" Godfrey shouted. "What are you doing here?" He threw the first ball of three into the gutter. The second hit one pin. He was understandably distracted. Binner still had the lead by a single point.

"Godfrey needs to hit one pin to win this match and advance to the final for the WCB title against Momchilo and Black Ninja Seven!"

As Godfrey approached the line to release the ball, Judy stood up and, touching Binner's arm, threw the nacho's into the back of Godfrey's head, causing him to lose footing and direction. The ball ended up in the gutter and Jordan Binner had won.

"It looks like Dale Godfrey choked, and Jordan Binner will advance against 'Hollywood' Dragan Momchilo and Black Ninja Seven for the WCB title!"

Godfrey was pissed. "Robert, did you know about this?"

"No, I'm sorry Dale. Just try to stay calm." Towell nodded to two security officers. Within seconds Godfrey was all rage and tried to tear through the plastic environment to get to Binner. Restrained by the security men, Godfrey was ordered out of the building by Towell.

Godfrey, swearing up a storm, had his hands pretzelled behind his back, and kicked with free limbs, spitting on the security guards, until the door locked behind him. The WCB cameras followed him down the street.

"Okay cut," Towell ordered.

Black Ninja Seven's wife Sarah was chatting up Clay Shallaghan, who had been flown in for a special musical consultation for a possible WCB CD that was scheduled for a 1998 release.

"So, how are you enjoying the scene back here?" Sarah asked.

"It's pretty intense. Robert might get me to score a few songs. I write music, so I'm trying to get a feel for the characters."

"That's interesting, what kind of music do you do?" Sarah said, running her soft fingers across Clay's knuckles.

"I'm in a couple of bands, and I produce some up-and-coming acts as well. I sort of dabble all over," Clay said, sipping a complimentary beer. Sarah smiled and stroked the top of Clay's hand. They talked and entwined, undetected within the mesh of hyper-masculine pursuits that bearded the rest of the building.

"Who are you rooting for?" Clay asked.

"I'm not sure," she answered with coy blue eyes, hiding her bag of Ninja merchandise which her husband had hoped to autograph.

Fresh from the shower, Momchilo noticed that some of his soccer scouts were in the stands and when he scanned the crowd closer, he also saw some of his soccer teammates whispering to each other, reaching for nachos with strings of melted cheese. Dragan lit a smoke and nodded. *Okay, I can do this, one more match, here comes Jerry's assistant, gonna tell me the idea... fuck my stomach, what is that, okay it's gone, no, it's back, felt that this morning too, on the bus.... Okay, here she comes, Jerry's assistant, her name is, Deb, sweaty Deb, details, she's going to give me details for the match.... Like the rules, like how I should react to the crowd.... Okay, relax, I'm doing good, I'm okay, I'm okay. Fuck I'm tired.*

Back under the welt of the overhead lights and calculated adrenaline, Towell snickered. "The final match to decide the fate of the undisputed WCB championship will be between Jordan Binner and Dragan

Momchilo and Black Ninja Seven in a triple-threat match. This should be something. We're going live to Dragan's dressing room."

With the cameras rolling, Jerry Tomlin stepped into the frame and introduced one of the finalists for the contest. "It's my pleasure right now to bring in 'Hollywood' Dragan Momchilo."

The camera filmed Momchilo in the mirror as he splashed cold water on his face and then dried it with a towel. A blurred Jerry Tomlin paced behind him as the interview began. "This is good," Robert Towell told the floor director. "Keep it going, it's raw, unhinged."

A cell phone rang; the assistant picked up and muttered back a few words before walking towards the challenger. A stagehand passed Momchilo the phone. "It's for you."

"Who is it?"

"I don't know."

"Hello? I'm at work. No, not that job, my other one. Never mind. No, I told you Mom, I didn't steal the sugar. No, I didn't. I have to go."

He hung up.

Jerry Tomlin: "Okay, Dragan, I don't mean to rush you but we have to start this interview."

"Okay Tomlin, fuck."

"Gus, let's roll."

The sun-gun illuminated the narrow jaw of the young Serb, and the final pre-match interview was underway.

"You saw the last match where Binner won by a single point. With everyone bowling at basically the same skill level, what will be your strategy for tonight's main event?"

"I just want to get through the night and leave with my head up," Momchilo said, and walked out of the shot.

"All right, 'Hollywood' Dragan Momchilo is on his way to lane sixteen, Robert, back to you."

"Folks you heard Momchilo, tonight is very personal, his family is watching worldwide. His mother has accused him on several occasions of stealing bags of sugar and giving them to his friends for their cottage, well today, Dragan could be bringing home a lot more than a bag of stolen sugar. He could walk away WCB champion! Mrs. Momchilo, I hope you're watching."

The match began in a friendly sportsmanlike show of skill, spares and strikes. At the beginning of the second frame, Black Ninja Seven took a swing at Momchilo, who ducked just as Binner joined the brawl. "Oh my, from behind, Binner with a knee to the lower back, and a push, Black

Ninja Seven has just been sent into that unforgiving wooden partition," Tomlin cried.

As the Ninja struggled, his hand caught in a section of wooden paneling, Binner approached with a bowling ball and landed the green sphere into the small of his back. Momchilo meanwhile bowled a frame of gutters for the Ninja who was now 20 points behind both men.

"Folks this one is all but over, for Binner and Momchilo, it's an even 80 points."

By the fourth frame, when Jordan Binner seemed poised to take over, Dragan was hinged on an inner turmoil, caught up in the anxiety of competition. His face seemed exposed and vulnerable, as if it was losing layers. Some women in the audience cheered sympathetically. Some rubbed their legs together like crickets.

"Let's finish him off," Binner said, hand extended to Momchilo. Within seconds both men stomped on Black Ninja Seven's shoulders and upper torso.

"Jordan Binner just spat in Momchilo's face!"

Temporary blinded by Slurpee and nicotine spit, Momchilo stammered in front of the fallen Ninja.

"I need this Dragan, I'm sorry." And with those casual words the confession turned into vengeance, as Binner threw an open bag full of sugar into Momchilo's eyes, temporary sending his opponent to the floor.

"Oh my God," Towell told the audience on pay-per-view, "this is insane, was that sugar? Folks we're not certain but it could very well be that Momchilo is out with the very sugar he was accused of stealing from his house moments ago."

"Fuck, Jordan, you asshole, I can't see."

Towell leapt up on his chair and continued to do play-by-play with apoplectic enthusiasm. "I'm sure his mother is at home enjoying this one." She was, but "didn't appreciate being mentioned on television at all," Momchilo would later tell *Inside Teen Sports*.

Jordan Binner continued his dominance in the final. He flipped up the table cloth of a nearby vendor's booth and pulled out a steel bat. "Oh my, Jordan told us backstage that he would do whatever it took to walk out of here a champion, but this, in my opinion, is going just too damn far."

The sound of the Ninja's back absorbing the repetitive steel hits was too much for some members of the live audience. A long stretcher appeared from backstage, with ample space for Black Ninja Seven, who was carefully lifted onto it. One of the ambulance attendants took the bat from the hand of Binner.

Jerry Tomlin: "Folks, it could be damage to the seventh vertebrae, the renal artery or the thoracic nerves, as Binner just did a number on Black Ninja Seven, right across the throat. As you can see in this replay, he moves from the throat to the exposed lower back, the upper torso, the quads, Binner is relentless, and now bat or no bat, seems poised to finish off this match."

Binner recalls: "I remember I had all this sugar on my hands and I was gonna wipe my eyes, and looked over at Dragan and he was like, trying to get back into the match, his eyes were all red and I looked over at Rob and he was just grinning and like totally supportive, the crowd was stirred up, and I remember stopping for a second and in the front row of the audience these three guys in suits were taking notes and whispering to each other. It was a great night for me, because I finally kinda understood what was happening around me, and I was young so I didn't really worry about consequences or like, oh no, what will people think. Later Rob told me that those men were producers of some bowling prime time shows.... I felt totally protected by WCB."

Momchilo took the extended arm of Binner and crashed it against the pillar, disarming the boy of his bag of sugar. As the Serbian youth scattered his tears, Binner kicked backwards, landing on the upper thighs a few times and on some exposed ribs.

> **"I REMEMBER THE SOUND WAS DEAFENING, AND THE CROWD WAS REALLY AFRAID, I JUST THOUGHT HE WAS GOING TO CUT SOMEONE."**
>
> **— JERRY TOMLIN**

Jerry Tomlin stood up as the action penetrated outside the confinement of lane sixteen. "This is no longer about standards and practices, this is a fight to the finish."

The camera crew had now dispersed into two small units: one for the action at lane sixteen, and one in the dank arteries of the bowling alley itself. A motorized sound began to wash over the crowd in a worrisome pitch. From an open window on the second floor, into a washroom and down through the fire stairwell entrance, Dale Godfrey emerged with a running chainsaw. The camera operator tumbled back into a corner, as if tripped up by the unexpected manoeuvre, capturing a shaky dose of Godfrey madness.

"The plucky Serb is back, arms flailing, trying to psyche out Binner, but Binner will have none of that, he's here to finish this game," Tomlin cried, his headphones slipping off his sweating skull.

Binner tried to connect with Momchilo's jaw, but was overpowered. "Momchilo has blocked it, leg sweep, and the back of Binner's head hit hard on that unforgiving alley wood. Momchilo is here to bowl, he's here for a fight and these fans are behind each punch, each block, and they are behind this Momchilo offensive!"

Dale Godfrey began to plough through the alley as Towell described the chaos. As he passed the WCB broadcast desk, Godfrey grabbed a nearby microphone and pointed at Binner, chainsaw still screaming. "Binner, I'm going to cut your balls off, and feed them to my new goldfish. You fucking prick!"

The crowd exploded in a confluence of jeers, laughter and bad grammar.

Robert Towell remembers: "A few mothers escorted their offspring to higher waters but overall,

throwing it in the air, and spinning around like a ballerina, and my Dad grabbed me by my shirt, pulled me off the field, drove me home, and never showed up to another game. Every other game I had to get a ride with a coach or a friend's Dad, or hitchhike. Years later, when I made it to the semi-professional level, I told my father, and he said to me, "When you were young I used to train you to follow in my footsteps but it was not your fate." My father had played for the Yugoslavian national team in the World Cup. He was given the North American soccer player of the year award by Pele in 1981. This was later when he was playing for the New York Cosmos. He got a watch that was worth $30,000 and I took it and wore it on a date when I was thirteen. On the back it was engraved.

YOUR FATHER AND MOTHER DIVORCED IN 1993. WHAT WERE THE CIRCUMSTANCES?

Dragan: Well if you must know, it's just, whatever, I got beat up a lot. I used to have to go out and pick my own branch. It's nothing that you would ever see in a Bell long distance commercial. So I guess I was out with a girl, on a date, in Ajax, Ontario of all places, and came home to police cars at my home with smoke coming from the windows, and a police officer told me that I could not go inside and that my father was being taken out by handcuffs and he had broken my Mom's rib cage and set the house on fire. And the next time I saw him was at the Whitby mental institute. When my Dad went up on trial, the entire Serbian community from church was on his side, and on my mother's side it was empty. My Mom won, custody I mean.

DRAGAN, YOUR FATHER WAS A PROFESSIONAL SOCCER PLAYER IN THE 1970S AND 1980S. HOW DID THIS INFORM YOUR EARLY CHILDHOOD ATHLETICISM?

Dragan: When I was four my father went to my first soccer game and put me on a team with eight year olds because when he was four he was playing with eighteen year olds, I mean, that's what he told me, that's what my sister told me. At one of these games, when I was four, I took the chalk line from the field and I was it may have been the only decent line that Godfrey had ever delivered."

Dragan Momchilo was now reaching for the ball return. "I can't see… fuck, I can't see shit…."

Tomlin improvised, "Momchilo is still not coherent, I don't know if he can finish this match."

The crowd was hostile, they wanted a result. Sensing a mood swing, Robert Towell stood up from the broadcast desk and tossed Momchilo a small bottle of eye drops. After applying several drops Momchilo's vision returned, as did his competitive prowess.

"A strike, a spare, a double-under hook, a stomp to the lower back of the fallen Ninja, you've got to hand it to 'Hollywood' Dragan Momchilo, a lesser athlete would have stayed down, and called it a night."

Still giving chase was Dale Godfrey, trying to corner Jordan Binner with the noisy saw. Binner cried to WCB promoter Robert Towell, pleading with the former child-star bowler.

"Jesus, this can't be scripted, Rob what am I suppose to do?"

"Yeah, like I'm going to stop a guy with a chainsaw. I'd run if I were you," Robert Towell said casually, popping a mint into his mouth.

Now terrified and without hope, Jordan Binner jumped up onto a nearby merchandise table. By this time, several security guards had cornered Godfrey, who was forced to put down the chainsaw which was obviously compromising his speed.

As the security team folded Godfrey into their possession, Robert Towell closed the segment: "Dale Godfrey has once again lost the match and his mind. This isn't a good career move. If Jordan can't come back to finish the match, our new champion will be Dragan Momchilo."

There was a horrifying song that slowly leaked into the PA system, a menacing choir, minced with explosive and metallic crashes. The lights began to flicker on and off, and the occasional cloud of smoke would cough into the main lane of action.

"Momchilo has guttered the rest of Binner's turns, he's won this tournament, he is the new champion of WCB!"

The announcer made it official: "Ladies and Gentlemen, here is your winner, and new undisputed champion, 'Hollywood' Dragan Momchilo!"

Some extra WCB hands came in and swarmed the youth, put him on their shoulders and handed him the championship trophy. Flashbulbs and confetti peppered the air, coupled with a quick round of indoor fireworks.

Backstage at BOWLBRAWL

On what was scheduled as a rare evening of salubrious pursuits, Martina Sorbara and Katherine Cockshutt found themselves involved in wine with the occasional handful of grapes, strawberries and cherries, while their soft tongues melted brie, a safe distance from the frothing bowling trenches.

"Katherine is a big slut," Martina teased, sipping on her glass of merlot.

"Fuck yeah, me a groupie, the inconsequential shit..." Katherine blathered. "Add all the numbers up... add up the whole thing, the fucking bowling spectacle, we're just rolling in attention now, Martina, did you see that last match?" Katherine slurred.

"You're already wasted, you dumb floozy. Katherine is a floozy."

"Everyone wants to be with us, we're all fucking the world," Katherine said, sloshing some of her red wine onto the floor.

"You fucked the Ninjas," Martina said with a cartoon giggle, one that seemed relaxed, without worry. Things were slow backstage, devoid of physical assault and the scent of the boorish audience.

WCB photographer Katherine Cockshutt with singer Martina Sorbara backstage at BOWLBRAWL, March 1997.

"I mean it was a bit much," Cockshutt added, "I was not exploited so much as completely drunk, like everyone else, and we talked to the media way too much." According to both, half the stories were made up from drunken nights on the road. "Like I really fucked two Ninjas, whatever...." The backstage area was prepped for a lush reception, a gold curtain was added to give the room a sense of prestige. A small motorized water fountain and a tropical fish tank were brought in for the post-match reception.

As the elite and heavily guarded entourage began to circle the buffet of imported chocolates and rivers of fine wine that were stocked and ready for the press and others, Katherine Cockshutt pulled Martina Sorbara into a corner with an anonymous member of the press. "That was crazy, this is crazy."

"Yeah Katherine, this is kind of nuts," Martina said, blowing her bangs from her dramatic brown eyes.

"Martina, *you* are kind of nuts. Come on let's get more wine." Katherine commanded.

"I'm nuts? At least I don't fuck Ninjas, you dirty slut."

"Yeah well, Ninja sex is awesome," Katherine said, nodding hello to Jerry Tomlin who was quick to undo his tie.

"Here comes your new man," Martina smirked.

"Shh. It's secret."

"Hi, I'm Martina."

"Hey, I'm Jerry, are you guys having a good time?"

"Yep. Martina has fun everywhere. She's thin, dialogue friendly."

"Good." Jerry Tomlin smiled, undoing a button and taking a sip of his wine.

Katherine pinched his arm slyly, leaned in, and completed with a sexy whisper, "Are you my good boy tonight?" Jerry's eyes locked on Robert and Nikola entering the room. Jerry turned his voice into a whisper which only Katherine could hear.

"No one here wants to fuck you like I do."

Fans who emailed WCB regarding the bad language used at BOWLBRAWL are getting the following reply: "Notwithstanding the 7 second delay from our live programming to telecast, last night's WCB program aired unacceptable language during a live segment, for which we apologize to our audience."

MANY REFERRED TO BOWLBRAWL AS "SUICIDE WATCH". WHY WAS THAT?

Dragan: It was the first pay-per-view of its kind. For us it was a make it or break it situation. It was suicide watch because everyone on that roster was willing to give their lives to make a name for themselves.

Robert: That's bullshit. Me and Tomlin dubbed it "suicide watch" when we were overseeing the editing of the VHS retail version because you fuckers were all suburban nightmares who were all like, ah, I feel so fucked-up, and have fucked-up values and fucked-up life dreams. Everything about each of you bastards was so self-destructive, passive aggressive and annoying, God, it just dragged on.... All you had to do was bowl and fight but you brought all your abandoned bullshit baggage with you. All that wasted footage, all those takes we had to do over and over again. Since when was sports emotional? Or sponsored by tobacco giants? How can you script people to be energetic when they're chain-smoking backstage worrying that someone named Billie-Joe, the assistant manager at Tim Horton's

#257, gave head to their best friend instead of them. Get your fucking priorities straight kids if you want to be a sports hero.

Greg: Well, simply put we wuz all getting tired of the contractual control Towell had over us. We even tried to cross media and were in negotiation to challenge the WBA with a showcase match with Mike Tyson but Towell and Don King corrupted that by trying to make it a feeding frenzy for network and cable TV. Those matches never took place, only faxes to offices. It would have been huge, but he was obsessed with keeping it underground so to speak, i.e. bowling or nothing. Hollywood and me only wanted Nickelodeon and the Disney channel. Check our hotel bills.

Robert: I've never talked to Don King. Don't try to make yourself sound important. Mike Tyson would have destroyed you. The only *Feeding Frenzy* I've ever heard of, is an adult film series involving, well, never mind. I never kept anything underground. I made us obvious. Idiots. It was you and Dragan who were repressed.

NIKOLA & ROBERT TOWELL'S APARTMENT

TORONTO, ONTARIO
MAY 12, 1997

As far as he could tell, the morning sun was entirely concealed behind the plush bedroom drapes, but Robert Towell would soon be able to touch it, like a newborn's limb, like the texture of fruit. He would open his mouth and breath it in, feel it course through his entire body. He cast an eye out his glorious bedroom window and hung up the phone, having checked messages from the office.

He walked back to Nikola, *semi-nude in bed, on cotton*, Robert liked to call her, as if she were a painting and he was writing copy for the museum hand-outs. "I just checked some of my messages at work. It seems ol' Dragan has a try-out with a semi-pro soccer team next week," Robert Towell said, fastening up his bathrobe, watching the back of Nikola's elbows.

"Dragan got a try-out for a professional soccer team?" Nikola said rolling her fishnet stockings up her blonde legs.

"Yeah, why?" Robert said.

"He must be strong," she winked, a teasing wink that came in three colours.

"Are you saying I'm a fat bastard?" Robert said, kneeing his way to her back on the bed.

"No, Rob, you're over-reacting," she said, removing his hands from around her neck.

"I see the way they look at you, like you're a thumbnail from a porn site, ready to be enlarged."

"That's a gross analogy."

"Listen, Dragan is a good soccer player, a natural athlete, but in my company he does what I tell him to."

"So who's supposed to win tonight?"

"I can't tell you that."

"Oh no?"

"But I can tell you one thing, keep up this Dragan has strength gimmick and I'll see you in court."

"Whatever Rob, I'm going to a business meeting now so I can't take any more of your abuse."

"Neither can I."

"What does that even mean?"

"It means, quit abusing me with your man-love for Dragan."

"I don't love Dragan. You need to stop living in this make believe world in which you think you created everyone and absorb all their attributes. You need to be more generous."

"Okay. We'll have a Christmas party this year, I promise."

"That's not what I mean."

Robert Towell picked up the phone and watched Nikola's ass snake out of the bedroom. He thumped his feet on the bed in a fit.

"Hey Jerry, it's Robert Towell."

"Hey. Everything okay? How's Nikola?"

"That's the trouble Jerry, I need to keep her in line, I think she doesn't

"I HAD A LOT OF RESERVATIONS, EVEN SLEEPLESS NIGHTS ABOUT GIVING HIM THAT HUGE PUSH. THE SIDE-EFFECT OF THIS PUSH HOWEVER WAS THAT THE TOBACCO COMPANIES LOVED HIS FACE, EVEN THOUGH I THOUGHT THE SMOKING WAS DOING OBVIOUS DAMAGE. HIS SKELETAL APPEARANCE WORKED WITH THE CAMERAS, AND THEY TOLD ME DRAGAN HAD A CERTAIN GLOW TO HIM. I THOUGHT THEY WERE TALKING RADIOACTIVITY. I WANTED HIM TO QUIT, BECAUSE THE ONLY TRUE FOCUS I EVER SAW IN HIS PHYSICAL MAKE-UP, WAS WHEN HE WAS LIP-LOCKED WITH A FILTER. BOWLING WAS, AT THE TIME, A SMOKER'S MARKET, I WAS WATCHING GOLF ONE AFTERNOON AND DIDN'T SEE A SINGLE CLOUD OF TOXINS, AND GOLF IS AN OUTDOOR SPORT. HIS FATHER, A FORMER PRO SOCCER CHAMPION, WAS REALLY TOUGH ON THE BOY. THERE WAS NO WAY FOR MR. MOMCHILO TO EVER PREDICT HE WOULD SEE THE DAY HIS SON'S SOCCER CLEATS TROD ONTO THE UNLIKELY SURFACE OF THE BOWLING LANE, BUT I HELPED THE STRAIN ON THE FATHER-SON RELATIONSHIP, I SOLIDIFIED IT, BECAUSE I THOUGHT IT WOULD MAKE DRAGAN A STRONGER MAN BUT IT JUST MADE HIM GO EVEN DEEPER INSIDE HIS OWN SLIMY CAVE OF THE SELF.

— ROBERT TOWELL

respect my authority."

"How can I help?"

He wanted Jerry to read his mind: *Say no more boss. You want me to write you a power ballad theme song for your next pay-per-view in which you reveal your true nature and power as the credits and company logo pop up on the screen and all fade to black, am I right?*

He spoke out loud, "Well, write me an anthem."

"I got your fax."

"If you need some music samples, I have some tracks laid down by Clay."

After the success he felt with the phone call, he tore into the kitchen and pulled out a plate containing half a pineapple. As he unwrapped it, he called for Nikola. She responded in a bedroom muffle. He began to count down from 10. "9... 8..."

"No Robbie, I don't have time to play," Nikola cried.

Brandishing the pineapple half, he chased her into the walk-in closet, but she escaped, until he cornered her in the kitchen near the cupboards, gently landing the juicy stump on her back.

"Robbie, I have to go to work."

"Call in pineapple."

They kissed juicily through the giggles and hair pulls of morning, slurping and sucking their way to a well-paced session of kitchen intercourse.

The curtains were misdrawn and stained with strawberry jam, like a sex crime photo shoot; slits of orange sun tried to lick at the corpses. As Katherine Cockshutt pet the back of Jerry Tomlin's neck, she let out a satisfied coo, wiped her hands off on her stomach and threw her head back on the pillow. If she had the energy, she would have been inspecting the haircut she had given herself earlier in the bathroom, something she couldn't stop talking about all morning. But Jerry had silenced her with sex, and the threat of another session was brewing as the two lazy executives lay, zombie-fucked in a Pennsylvania trance.

As she stretched and yawned, Jerry Tomlin snuck kisses in her mouth. She wanted to be on her feet, rolling up the new WCB posters but was confronted by his morning erection.

They both stared at the posters, which were slightly eclipsed by his hard on. "They look good don't you think?" Jerry said, lighting a cigarette.

She sprang out of the bed and carefully rolled the posters up and inserted them into plastic bags. She giggled and sipped the remainder of her bottled water. "Yeah, they do. I like them a lot," Katherine said. "What are you doing for the rest of the day?"

"Writing a theme song for Rob. How's Martina?"

"She's fine."

"Is she excited about singing the national anthem at the pay-per-view?"

"I guess so. She doesn't really *get* the whole WCB thing though, it's not really her scene."

"Yeah, it's not a lot of people's scene," Jerry Tomlin replied, edging himself closer to her naked back. "But I've known Rob a long time, you know?"

"Well, I like it, I mean, I watch the shows when I can, I try to get my girlfriends to watch it with me, I look for you, it's a little game that I have."

"I bet you do."

Jerry Tomlin looked at his day planner and his watch. From the corner of his eye he saw Katherine let her blouse fall to the ground, leaving her back exposed and pure in the morning light. As he approached her, his cell phone rang. He kept walking, the sheet falling from his body. He saddled up to her with all the momentum of a Viking, a cave bear, and a starved hillbilly unbuckling his overalls, heading for the nearest bale. He let it ring.

Do Not Stand In The Way Of My Inevitable Victory
(Robert Towell theme song)

WORDS BY JERRY TOMLIN / MUSIC BY CLAY SHALLAGHAN

I am the man / I am your boss / I am the one you cannot cross / I am the power / I am the glory/ I am the one / the only man / who murdered bowling. / You work for me / you live and breathe / you cannot see / without me / pointing the way. / I am the man / I am your boss / I am the man you cannot cross. / Tiny maggot in my hand / tiny maggot see those fans? / They cheer for you / they make you breathe / they will not leave / until I squeeze / their pockets and dreams. / I plant you like a seed / then throw you this feed. / I am the man / I am your boss / I am the one you cannot cross / I am the power / I am the only / dirty bastard / who murdered bowling.

SEPARATION: The distance you allow between your standing position and where you want the ball placed on the lane to hit the target.

SHADOW BALL: A ball rolled in practice without the pins being set, usually just one or two balls before competition play.

SHORT PIN: A pin rolling on the alley bed which fails to reach and hit a standing pin.

SHOTGUN SHOT: Rolling the ball from the hip.

It was 4:15 PM when Robert Towell exited the taxi and noticed Jerry Tomlin pacing in front of a rental van. He sped up his walk and waved to Tomlin who was in some sort of netherworld.

"Hey, so, are we set?"

"Yeah, I've got the merch, and…"

"Tell me the keys are ready…"

"Rob, the alley keys are at the realtor's office."

"Great. What time can I pick them up? I just got off the phone with my lawyer, the deed has been signed and faxed in."

"He said any time."

"Let's go. Great, good," Robert Towell said, scanning the back of the van. "You have the extra Lebelle merch, okay, is it priced?"

Jerry Tomlin was gaining a reputation backstage as the go-to-guy. He was calm, and unlike Towell, totally direct and sincere.

Even though he wasn't on the card, Robert Towell wanted to push the Greg "Agamemnon" Lebelle merchandise in the States because there was no hiding the fact that WCB had huge plans for the big guy.

"There are two more boxes of shirts and posters at the hotel room," Jerry Tomlin said, distracted, tapping on the clipboard he was holding, which seemed to slow everything down.

"So," Tomlin said, brushing Towell's arm, "you really bought this bowling alley then?"

Towell nodded. "It was cheap. Got it at an auction. Nikola tipped me off about it. Fuck it's crazy, so much shit going down right now, you know I'm just not clear-headed, never have been but man, I just came from the

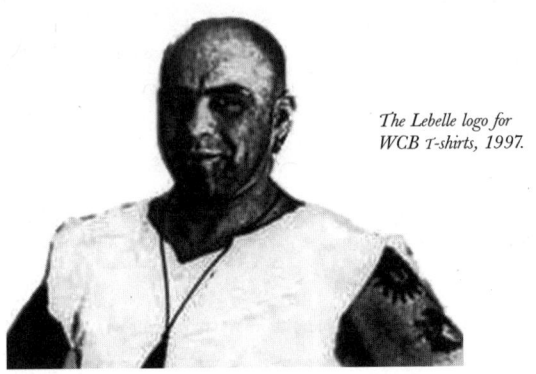

The Lebelle logo for WCB T-shirts, 1997.

radio station to give away one hundred seats."

"Give away?" Tomlin balked. There had been a few issues about give-aways, and the board was wary of this new trend.

"Trust me, I want a controlled amount of spectators. We sort of sprang this idea on the world, didn't we? I mean, I just got the alley secured today, have to make sure there are at least some people in the frame up, right?"

"Yeah, it's just that if we'd postponed it for two weeks, we could have sold more tickets."

Towell shook his head: "And make sure you get extra security, and that the fire department is on call in the lot. It's going to be messy, but great footage for our promos and VHS. It'll really fuck up the PBA's ratings that's for sure. Up to now they haven't been able to gauge what we've been up to, but with this release, it's all over."

"What can I say Rob, that's sick." Tomlin smiled, impressed to the gills.

Now veterans in the art of guerrilla set-up and tear-down, the sparse WCB crew worked their magic, and by 8:00 PM the cameras were rolling for a limited online telecast. A lot of pre-arranged fire-enhancing chemicals were pungent in the alley. So cruel and pressing were these vapours that Towell, ever the compassionate promoter, lit an immense amount of incense backstage, and even brought in some fans which he'd bought at a local hardware store, to help the scent spread.

As for coverage in the greater Niagara region, a few local news stations were allowed to film excerpts for their sports recaps later that night on the evening broadcast. Otherwise it was exclusively a WCB brand telecast, just the way Towell wanted it.

The pay-per-view began with a long shot of the U.S. flag hanging from the rafters. Another camera panned down from the rafters onto the WCB desk where Jerry Tomlin opened the show with his colleague Jordan Binner. "Folks welcome to WCB INVASION. I'm Jerry Tomlin, along with Jordan Binner who came oh so close to becoming champion at BOWLBRAWL, just two months ago."

"That's right Jerry," Binner said with a slight knot of regret in his facial expression. "But I'm training and I'll be back in the thick of things soon, but now, what a night of bowling we have in store for the fans of WCB."

"Robert Towell has a special message for the crowd here in Buffalo, for our first ever, U.S. pay-per-view," Jerry Tomlin continued the hook, "and I think it's up next."

The camera followed Robert Towell walking backstage towards the curtain, smug and confident, patting the sides of his hair, barely making contact with the perfect arrangement of follicles. The arena erupted as the owner passed through the curtain, Jordan Binner piped up over the arena cheers: "Robert Towell is making his way now to the centre of the bowling alley and he's wearing a black cape!"

Towell nodded knowingly to the fans, as if he were absorbing their approval. He stopped at the lip of lane sixteen where the WCB logo and championship trophy stood on a display case.

Towell began: "Ladies and gentlemen, it is an honour to present to you, for the first time in the Unites States, the undisputed WCB champion, Dragan Momchilo."

With that introduction, a short-lived series of indoor fireworks peppered the arena light blue and pastel pink with streaks of yellow, cueing "Hollywood" Dragan Momchilo, who was not wearing his athletic gear, but wore street clothes. Robert waited until the champion was toe to toe with him, and continued: "All right," he said, shaking the champion's hand, followed by a nod to the crowd. "All right," he continued, extending his hand to the crowd, urging without words, the champion to acknowledge their cheers. "Dragan, you won the WCB championship at our last pay-per-view, BOWLBRAWL, back in Canada, and tonight, we are going to start your reign in style. Tonight, you will be competing against Buffalo's local legend Gary Dribbs in a 4-alarm match. But this isn't going to be a big brawl, after all, we're here in Buffalo, known for its civility. No, we are going to have a match up that is based on, believe it or not, actual skill.... But of course, there will be a bit of a twist."

"Rob, I'm ready for anything. Thanks for having me here, and it's an honour to represent WCB here in the United States. I want to thank all my fans for their letters, from all over the country, but Rob, what the fuck is a 4-alarm match?"

"Well, you'll see. The rules are simple, but first let's introduce your opponent, local legend Gary Dribbs."

A chorus of cheers drifted into the lane as Dribbs wallowed onto the scene, looking a bit out of sorts. Whatever accolades Dribbs had secured in the sport were not apparent in the way he moved. His body language begged for isolation, simplicity, and at best, a good afternoon nap. Parading in a proper burgundy crested bowling top with an exaggerated collar, hair oil-slicked back, Gary Dribbs, ranked 14th in New York State, walked towards lane sixteen. Towell waved the local veteran over with a campy smile, one which bordered on vulture, or even pterodactyl. The crowd was pumped up, due to some near-lethal bowling trailers featuring the WCB's recent ratings swell, and highlights from past pay-per-views.

In an interview before the match, Dribbs, filmed outside of a retirement village, promised to bring pride back to the tradition. "These so-called bowlers get me and the other boys really upset, what they're doing is wrong."

But now a slingshot of slang splattered the boom mics, as the converted WCB crowd jeered at Dribbs' meagre standing, preferring the new brand of hyper-masculine recruits.

Dribbs stood beside the WCB champion, nodding, but not accepting the champion's extended hand. The nervous energy was contagious; bad vibes drilled themselves invisibly into the aging building.

"Hello Gary, welcome to World Championship Bowling."

"Thank you Mr. Towell," Dribbs said, speaking nervously into the microphone.

"Now gentlemen, this match is for the undisputed WCB championship, and the winner will be the first bowler to score four strikes. It isn't total points, but whoever gets four strikes first will win the WCB title. Now, to make it fun, each time one of you gets a strike, there will be a small alarm. Also, because this is World Championship Bowling, and we are at the cutting edge of bowling telecasts, at the start of each frame, another lane will ignite. So for example, at the top of the second frame, lane eleven will ignite. At the top of the third frame, lane twenty will ignite, and so on, until we reach the tenth frame, so really boys, you should try to get those strikes by the fifth frame at the least, I mean, you don't want us all to die in this inferno do you?"

"This is crazy, I didn't agree to this," said Dribbs in protest.

"Fine, I guess that's what happened to your career, you choked, you knew that you were washed up, couldn't hack it. Dragan I guess you win by..."

"No, I'll do it, you can't come here from Canada and start insulting me, in my home town."

"Well, that was the idea," Robert Towell said clearly into the microphone, sneering into the camera. "Let's get this thing started, ring the bell."

The match began with local legend Gary Dribbs getting a spare, followed by Dragan Momchilo besting the situation with a strike. "Momchilo leads it 1-0, and there's that alarm we were promised," Jerry Tomlin reported from laneside, joined by Towell. "Things are going to get hot in here, and fast Jerry," said Jordan Binner with enthusiasm.

Jerry Tomlin recalls: "We had doused the lane in a bit of kerosene, which works just as well as that wax stuff that you're suppose to use to buff the alley." As the second frame started, the long shiny strip of lane eleven ignited. The gasps from the crowd complemented the unpredictable sounds of flame digesting the age-old wood.

"This is going to be the most controversial championship match I have ever witnessed," Jerry Tomlin gushed, watching Robert Towell smile uncontrollably off-camera. Jerry scanned the crowd, security guards were posted at each exit, and there was a first-aid stand set up behind the crew, and a large pitcher of water.

Gary Dribbs scored a strike, but in his second attempt, Dragan could only equal Dribbs's spare of the first frame.

"It's all tied up at 1, this has got to be a pressure cooker for both men," Jordan Binner told the folks at home.

The flames made the alley hot, and by the fourth frame, both athletes were sweating. "Folks, it looks like business is about to pick up, the champion is here to fight."

Despite warnings from Brunswick, WCB was giving free props to the company's new line of products. Jerry and Robert joked back and forth during the opening frames of the inferno match. "I believe that's a 12 pound Storm X Factor Vertigo and Dragan is using his standard Columbia Backyard Bully, I believe a 10 pound. I like the use of the Brunswick BVP Nemesis Black/Orange especially in today's inferno match," Tomlin said with a smug confidence. "What kind of wristband are today's bowlers wearing Robert?"

"Well, it's the pride of the pro circuit, the Brunswick Deluxe Wrist Band with metal insert in the back of the glove which provides comfort and support to your hand. We'll see how that benefits the players today during the hand-to-hand combat."

Dragan moved fast, managing two back to back strikes and began pouring on the insults. This, coupled with the growing cheers for the champion in the crowd, made it hard for Gary Dribbs to concentrate.

Momchilo was now ahead by one strike (3-2) having gained some momentum. "Momchilo seems impervious to that smoke," Jerry said, with a cloth muzzling his words.

The alley was virtually swallowed in flame and smoke, the audience exited quietly as the two bowlers struggled to complete the match. The announcers had to leave as well, but Towell stayed, filming what he could using a leaf blower to help clear some of the smoke.

The smoke dragged Momchilo into a domestic nightmare: his father's frustration as he kept running into the kitchen to get more matches, because his wife wouldn't stay lit. With a cigarette in his mouth Momchilo held tight to the sickening feeling of the memory as he thumbed for his lighter. Despite the darkness of his thoughts, he could not avoid the bright reality of the moment. As the ambulance attendants revived Dribbs Momchilo noticed Towell standing on top of the snack bar counter in his long black cape, laughing.

The following transcript was excerpted from an audio tape marked:
"Hunters / Underbelly Interview 2001"

"This fella named Towell, Rob Towell, started changing the game oh I say about 97, with that Invasion crap, where he humiliated Dribbs and slowly made all us regular fellas look fat and old and bald. Soon we couldn't even go to league night without people laughing at us. He made us all feel ashamed. Used to be our joy. Then, them thin folks come on the television there, with their muscles and their T-shirts and merchandise. The rates went up to bowl, he got all these licensing deals and the decent bowling alleys in town went under. Some of us even went off and hung ourselves. Fuck them scrawny pretty boy bowlers, with their slick logos and flashy entrance music. Fuck all of em, they ruined my life. My wife left me for one of them macho muscle pukes. You writing something about Towell? Tell him I'll see him and his bowlers in Hell. The day he gone and started WCB was the funeral of all of us combined, no decent folks left. No heart left. No game. Fuckin' Towell ruined it, ruined us. My hair is gone, it won't return."

"Ah quit your bitching Hank and check your barrels, don't want any mistakes like last time. No loaded equipment until we reach the underbelly proper...."

GREG LEBELLE'S APARTMENT

TORONTO, ONTARIO
MAY 26, 1997

The bachelor apartment of Greg "Agamemnon" Lebelle smelled of bleach and cleaning products.

"I'm cleaning, Dragan's over, just chilling out, long week," he told his bowling boss over the stretch of cord and the noise of a high-powered suburban vac.

"All right, if you want to meet up later, Jerry and I are going for drinks at Thermos before dinner at Flashlight. If you want to come by around 3:00 PM, we'll still be there."

"We'll see, not sure, I'm pretty beat."

"Nikola and I are going to have a late dinner on a boat, I think we're going to eat clouded perch, which is basically just perch with mashed potatoes."

"Sounds great, talk to you soon." Greg Lebelle hung up the phone and exhaled into the toxic apartment air.

He sat without a shirt, topless, fresh from another volunteer shift at a homeless shelter where he had been making appearances, not so much as a celebrity bowler, but out of a haunted need to help people. It was somewhat of a spiritual return, something his physical make up of piercings and tattoos seemed unable to offer. His monstrous frame and large shoulders eclipsed the back of the couch.

Meanwhile, in his own constant orbit of dementia, Dragan Momchilo paced back and forth in the kitchen unable to calm down with cigarettes or coffee, perhaps unaware the adrenaline from these substances would not illicit relaxation.

"So what you wanna watch?" Lebelle said, flipping past a blur of obnoxious wrestlers in a ring.

"Wait, go back for a sec."

"I'm not watching that aged Hogan."

"Did I ever tell you about this one time when I was out with my Dad and I was like six, and going on about Hulk Hogan this and Hulk Hogan that," Dragan said, mid-puff, mid-sip. "Anyway my Dad snapped at me, *Why do you spend so much time thinking about Hulk Hogan, it's not like he's sitting around at his house thinking about you.*"

Greg laughed. "Your Dad sounds like a great man."

Dragan began tucking his sweater deep into his pants and made certain Greg caught him in the act. Later, he would reveal to close friends, he did it to infuriate Greg, who would repeatedly tell him how awful he looked. "So you know, I read the reason Hulk Hogan has adopted the name *Hollywood* Hogan is because he has to pay royalties to Marvel Comics. True. When he started out they billed him as the Incredible Hulk Hogan."

"Why do you know all this fucking crap? Why Hollywood Hogan anyway?" Greg said, noticing the excessively tucked in sweater of his coworker.

"I think it's cause he lives there now, and he's an actor."

"His movies suck."

"He's too old."

"You want some more pop? There's some in the fridge."

"Sure."

"You hungry? Cause the Agamemnon sure is, we could get wings."

"I got no money."

"You got no money?"

"Seriously."

Dragan fiddled nervously with a cigarette package in his backpack and whatever he could find on Greg's coffee table.

"How's the home life?" Greg asked, still channel surfing.

"My family sees me with this bag, and in Serbia, if you wore a backpack it was to collect fire wood, they called you beggar boy. So that's what they call me when I come home with my bag on."

"How was Buffalo?"

"Good, too bad you couldn't come."

"I told you, I'm not allowed in the States."

Dragan began to tuck in his sweater again. "What are you doing?" Lebelle said, almost swallowing an unlit cigarette.

"I'm getting ready for the protest," Dragan said.

"In that outfit?"

"Greg, it's my heritage."

"Well can you not leave your heritage around my apartment, I came home last week and that crappy Serbian folk music was blasting. Do you dance around in here naked with that stuff cranked?"

"No. We go to this Serbian club after the protests."

"Hand it to the Serbs. You guys are real organized."

SIDEBOARDS: Vertical division between lanes at the pit end.

SIXPACK: Six strikes in a row.

SLEEPER: A pin directly behind another pin; respectively: 8-4, 5-1, 9-3.

SLICK: Land condition highly polished; tends to hold back hook. Not the same as oily.

SLIDE: The last step of the delivery.

SLOT ALLEY: Lane on which strikes come easy caused by a track worn into the lane.

World Championship Bowling and its carnival rolled into the O'Connor Bowl at the edge of East York at approximately 4:00 PM to set up. The company now boasted a road crew of fifteen men and thirteen women, three different vendors: one was a local company that did T-shirts, one was from Vancouver who specialized in photographs and calendars, and a third from Detroit who had secured the company's action figure contract, did some U.S. licensing for video games, and was in development for a possible cartoon spin-off.

"How are we doing at the gate?" Robert Towell said, taking a portfolio from Jerry Tomlin's hand.

"Fine," Tomlin said.

"These the latest figures?"

"Yep."

"It's about 1750 bucks, last time I checked, we should clear about 3000 which is big. I mean, people are coming into this place by the busloads."

The opening match was a dismal but clean affair between local league champion Frank Cosco and Black Ninja Six. Cosco was brought in as part of a plan to lure actual bowling fans to WCB events.

"Here is your winner, Frank Cosco," said the lane announcer.

In his cotton prison, Black Ninja Six hung his head in shame and walked back to the dressing room area, unravelling his mask and undoing his cloth belt. Katherine Cockshutt was chatting with Black Ninja Seven and looked up. As Six slowly meandered back, his face said it all.

"How did it go?" Katherine asked.

"What a horrible night," he said, throwing his mask to the ground.

Pampered in his director's chair, and dressed in a referee outfit, Robert Towell relished the moment, nodding to the Ninjas and Katherine as they passed the make-up area. Towell smiled, visually digesting his ongoing bowling lab spectacle. He could feel it growing, it was an energy now.

Back at the WCB broadcast desk, Dale Godfrey and Jerry Tomlin prepared for the next match.

"Wow, that was a great match, wouldn't you say Jerry?"

"It was a helluva contest, both men gave it their all."

"What's next?" Godfrey said, scratching his curly uncombed hair, his eyes, dark brown, never blinked. He was wearing a Dallas Cowboys winter coat that made a lot of noise against the microphone when his chin ruffled the foam of the mouthpiece. When Godfrey turned to cough, the world heard the NFL rayon slice into the broadcast.

"Folks, if you are just joining us, you're in for a treat. Lebelle versus Momchilo for the undisputed title, and Robert Towell is the guest referee!"

> **"THAT PAY-PER-VIEW BEGAN WITH SEVERAL LOW-BUDGET COMMERCIALS SELLING EVERYTHING FROM BLOCKS OF PINK ICE TO RADIAL TIRES AND EXTRA SMALL SPOONS FOR PEOPLE WITH LARGER DENTAL ARRANGEMENTS."**
> — ROBERT TOWELL

With that announcement the sparks flew and the in-house pyrotechnics spackled the inner gum line of the O'Connor Bowl, a sister alley to the Thorncliffe Bowlerama who didn't, according to licensing agreement, pick up the rights to BOWLBASH in time.

A strange record scratch sample began to leak from the speakers, followed by a series of chains rattling in an echoing hallway. The lights in the bowling alley shut off, and an eerie yellow glow spooked out of the ventilation system. Slowly the song grew in tenacity:

I am the man, I am your boss, I am the one you cannot cross.

More chains, thuds, and a bit of a guitar cackled out, then the heavy techno drums swelled, slashing the building, creating a churning worry for those who were industry-obsessed. These were the fans Towell loved. The song provided hives of an eerie presence, this was Towell's theme song, and as he walked towards lane sixteen in referee attire, the sneer on his face said it all, he was the boss. This was no hobby, this was his sport, and somewhere he had the paperwork to prove it.

I am the power. I am the glory, I am the one, the only man, who murdered bowling.

"Dale, by the looks of things, this night will mark the beginning of the corporate agenda of one Mr. Robert Towell."

You work for me, you live and breathe, you cannot see without me, pointing the way.

"I'm just glad that I have a job in the WCB offices now," Jerry Tomlin said. "I'm glad I don't have to deal with Towell on the same level as say, someone like Black Ninja Seven, what about you Dale?"

"Well, Towell is getting stronger every day, he wants to be the biggest bowling company, and he could succeed."

I plant you like a seed, then throw you this feed, I am the man I am your boss, I am the one you cannot cross, I am the power I am the only, dirty bastard, who murdered bowling.

Robert Towell took the microphone as his theme song waned into the background and the bowling buzz resumed. "Ladies and Gentlemen, I'd like to introduce you to the special time keeper, my wife, the lovely Nikola Towell!" Nikola Towell began her soft parade from the backstage curtain towards lane sixteen where Robert Towell stood in the black and white T-shirt which symbolized his referee duties for the evening's main event.

Nikola Towell – in a sinewy Kokosolaki number, all knotted sheaths and missing fabric – smiled as she walked surrounded by four security officers. Towell winked at the booth and flexed his arms for the crowd.

Jerry Tomlin and Dale Godfrey sat at the WCB desk in front of lane sixteen. Tomlin nodded to the folks at home, noting the red light of camera three was now focused on him.

"Folks it looks like Towell's in rare form tonight, but who does he favour in this main event? I mean, this is it, these men have never faced one another, what's going to happen?"

"I think it's going to get ugly, real quick Jerry," Godfrey said, scratching the top of his toque.

"Ladies and gentlemen, now making his way to lane sixteen, he is the challenger, and number one contender for the WCB championship, weighing 224 pounds, Greg 'Agamemnon' Lebelle!" After the introduction the house lights went off. On three screens the WCB logo appeared.

Lebelle stood and smoked patiently, awaiting the champion. The screen filled up with pre-recorded footage of the Towells backstage argu-

ing. "Rob, don't be stupid, I was just saying how impressed I was that Dragan is playing soccer on top of being WCB champion," Nikola could be heard saying.

Robert, standing with his back to the camera, muttered and rocked back and forth in both rage and insecurity. "Oh is that right? Well who is running this company and making everything happen, designing T-shirts, booking autograph sessions and approving action figures? Santa Claus? Jesus? No, it's me, Robert Towell, the boss. So stop it, this is my company. You work for me."

"Rob, I'm your wife, I'm just trying to take an interest in what you do and who you work with."

"Interest? So now you're interested in Dragan? Are you interested in anyone else? Maybe you want a Ninja to come over next weekend while you're swimming and he can wash the car? Would you like that? In his little ninja swimsuit?"

"Rob, I have to go to my car to get something. Calm down, eat a club sandwich, they're in season, as you would say."

The end of the segment showed "Hollywood" Dragan Momchilo on a soccer field with the sun setting over the WCB championship trophy.

Back at the broadcast desk, Jerry Tomlin shook his head in anticipation. "This is going to be a personal night, these three men are really under each other's skin."

"I'm just glad I'm here with you, and not in this match," Godfrey said.

"Here comes the champion now," Jerry Tomlin said, watching Momchilo enter from the back.

The dirtiest players in the game were frothing at the opportunity to showcase their abusive friendship in front of a live television audience.

"Dragan, you're fucking toast, I'm going to destroy you."

"I don't think so Greg, I'm on a roll."

The match started out clean until Lebelle orchestrated a brief run-in during the fourth frame and threw two gutters during Momchilo's turn.

"Towell, you going to do something about that?" Momchilo asked, cocking an eyebrow.

"Cheat to win, you do it back to him, that's not such a big infraction."

"Fuck this," he said, and as Lebelle prepared to open the fifth frame, the champ dropped a ball right on Lebelle's foot causing the big man to release his own ball and clasp his hands around his toes.

"Yeah, you want to start playing dirty? We haven't even reached the halfway mark."

"Yes we have you Hollywood idiot," Lebelle shouted back. "This is the final frame."

Towell stepped in and began shouting at Momchilo. The prison stripes of his referee shirt bumped against the champ's frame.

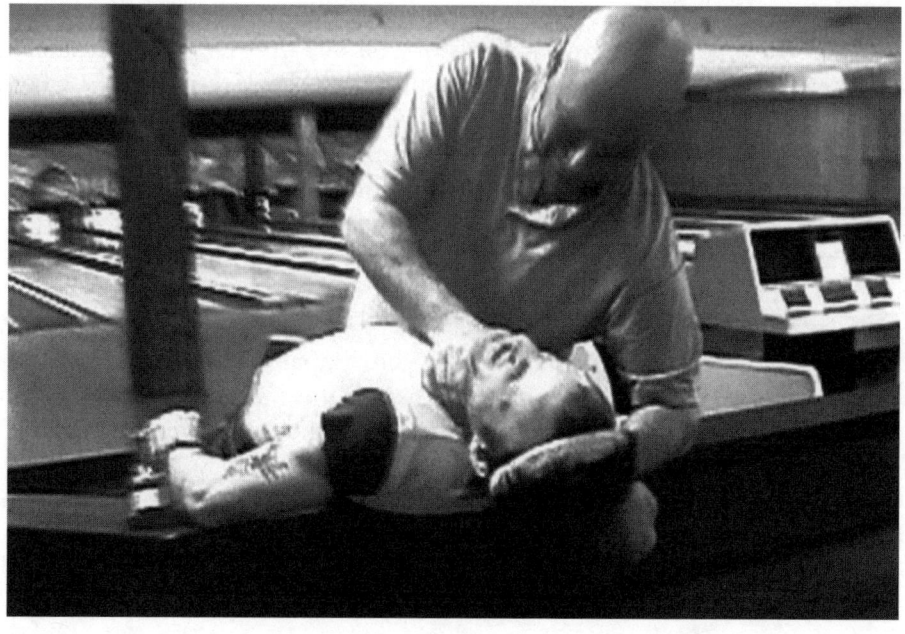

"Why are you yelling at me?" he retorted, his face flush against Towell's arms.

"I told you, watch it Momchilo," Towell said, grabbing his superstar by the throat, "this isn't soccer, this is WCB, this is where you make your living, so no more unsportsmanlike maneuvering."

"But Towell, you saw what he did," Momchilo protested, looking to the crowd for sympathy. The crowd booed Towell, but cheered for both competitors. The challenger, Greg "Agamemnon" Lebelle, sensing momentum, worked up the crowd with a series of facial close-up grimaces to the camera.

There were Dragan marks in the audience, those hanging on his every move. You could hear them tearing their vocal cords, but some preached specifics, including Cindy Pears from Ottawa: "He's the only natural athlete in the company, he plays soccer too, I looked up his name on the Internet. His Dad was like the best soccer player in the world for a bit."

"From Slovenia or something," the man next to Cindy added. "He's totally got to win tonight," the fan said, clutching her BOWLBASH programme.

"Folks, Dragan Momchilo is ahead now by nearly a dozen points, Greg Lebelle looks tired, and Towell is ready to pounce on the next person who makes an infraction, but he keeps looking backstage."

"Maybe he ordered some food."

"Oh shut up Godfrey, this is the main event, Towell's got better things to do than order food, something's going down," Tomlin insisted.

"Hey Rob, looks like I've got this one all tied up," Dragan Momchilo said with bravado. The crowd was behind him, and Towell knew what they would do for their champion, and he hated it.

Greg Lebelle began to charge the champion but the young Serbian leapt up onto the ball return and jumped over the incredible bulk, landing on top of Towell who had crept up onto the lane's lip to get a better look at the conflict.

"Oh shit, Towell's going to get pissed now."

Greg Lebelle dug deep into his pants and pulled out a grey-haired wig.

"Hey Dragan, guess who I am? I'm your Baba." Lebelle turned to the closest camera operator who sprinted towards the giant. Lebelle, tried out his best Eastern-European grandma voice: "Dragan, why did you take the sugar from us?"

Dragan Momchilo picked up a folding chair and threw it towards Lebelle. The chair landed on his foot. Lebelle shrugged it off.

"What are you doing Greg? You don't even look like my grandmother.

And why have you been posting anti-grandma promos all week on the Internet?" Momchilo blurted out, trying to focus on the frame.

Lebelle picked up the chair, throwing the wig to the crowd. As Momchilo turned his attention away from Lebelle, Towell took him by the throat and splattered him against the iron railing of the small snack area beside the announcer's table. From his pocket he pulled a shiny pair of handcuffs which dangled like earrings in the arena light.

"What are you doing?" Momchilo shouted, his hands and arms swarming in all directions, only to have his throat clogged by Towell's foot. "I'll break your jaw and all your precious dental work if you don't shut up."

"What the hell Rob... let me finish this match, it's the championship."

"Tonight you're finished," Towell said, throwing the cuffs onto his arm and flicking the cold metal across one of the iron bars.

With that Black Ninja Seven came out from the back and threw a heavy net over the cuffed champion.

"The champion is the victim of some supreme team-up, this plot is not going to sit well with this live crowd."

"Rob, come on, this is stupid," Momchilo said as Towell tossed the Ninja another set of handcuffs. "Do his ankles," instructed Towell. "Dragan this isn't stupid. This is WCB, and you work for me!"

Greg Lebelle smiled and picked up the wig from the fan who had caught it. After putting it on his head, he looked down at his captured opponent: "Hey, Dragan this one's for your grandma," Lebelle said, laughing as he posed, arms flexing, causing a ripple of giggling by those at laneside.

It was the final frame, and Lebelle threw an unjust gutter for the young champion. The computer registered a cruel zero.

"What a way to lose a match, and not only a match, but the undisputed WCB championship," Tomlin said from his broadcast position.

Lebelle finished Momchilo's remaining frames gently donating gutterball after gutterball as the young Serb struggled to stop the ultimate betrayal. Robert Towell's back was turned to Lebelle who finished the game with a spare.

"Folks, things have gone terribly wrong tonight for WCB champion 'Hollywood' Dragan Momchilo. In my opinion, this is not right," Jerry Tomlin said in shock.

The announcer made it official. "Here is your winner by a score of 122-93, and NEW undisputed WCB champion, Greg 'Agamemnon' Lebelle!"

Robert Towell handed over the WCB championship trophy to Lebelle and raised his giant paw in victory just as Towell's new theme song began to play.

As the show went off the air and WCB trademark and copyright information appeared at the bottom of the screen, the shot switched from Towell and Lebelle's celebration to the netted former champion spitting with hate.

NOTES ON BOWLBASH FROM 1BOWLING.COM

Robert Towell held a huge meeting backstage with the WCB talent roster yesterday before the tapings. The exact same thing that was said at the mid-card meeting was repeated again and Robert referred to us as "Internet critics" and "dirt sheets". Robert said what was going on absolutely disgusted him and said that if he finds out who is talking to the people on the Internet, he will, "fire them on the spot".

Greg Lebelle spoke up at the meeting and backed up Robert. He told a story about how he was recently doing an interview and some questions about future booking plans were asked. Lebelle stood right behind Robert and joked that, "If I see anybody on the Internet, I'll kill them and their grandmothers," which got a laugh from both the talent and crew.

The bowlers were also critiqued during the meeting; some felt it was less about being critiqued and more about being "publicly humiliated" in front of their peers. There were even some members of management that didn't agree with the idea of criticizing bowlers in front of the others. Needless to say, a lot of the talent is not looking forward to these meetings being a weekly occurrence.

In the speech in which Towell referred to Internet reporters as "parasites", he expressed some confusion as to why his superstars would talk to the press and reveal storylines. He was said to be very upset about the fact that the backstage meetings have been getting press as of late. It was said to be a very intense meeting for about forty-five minutes. Robert Towell was quoted as saying, "it ruins the illusion" and "spoils the product for the fans."

Robert Towell doesn't realize that much of his talent is upset and they talk to the press in hopes of a change. From what we have been told, the guys who are "top notch" (the ones being pushed) agreed with Robert. That should come as no surprise.

Bruce C. Dumair has not been at any tapings for several weeks because he is dealing with personal issues. Right now, David Lagana is wearing the Black Ninja Seven outfit in his place. Dumair had wanted to rework his character. One bowler backstage overheard Tomlin and Towell laughing, saying, "Dumair, you're the consummate light-hearted baby face. We can send you out there with a chainsaw and you can cut off both of Greg Lebelle's arms, and the fans just wouldn't believe it." No word on when Dumair will be back in the ninja gear. Also, there have been rumours that on more than one ocassion, Black Ninja Six has been played by an unnamed 17-year old female rugby player.

FROM WCB.COM

Last night at Cornwall's Bowling Palace, WCB owner Robert Towell announced that Ted Dawson would be facing newly crowned WCB champion Greg Lebelle at the upcoming pay-per-view GUTTER WARS in Ajax. After Dawson was introduced to the Cornwall audience, Greg Lebelle hit the scene and delivered this promo:

"What do I have to do to get you people to understand? So what, Dragan's injured? Playin' soccer? Buying bags of sugar for his fuckin' family? Towell you pathetic little bitch, you have to bring this piece of crap hick into WCB? Like bowling fans are gonna tune in to watch this has-been trailer

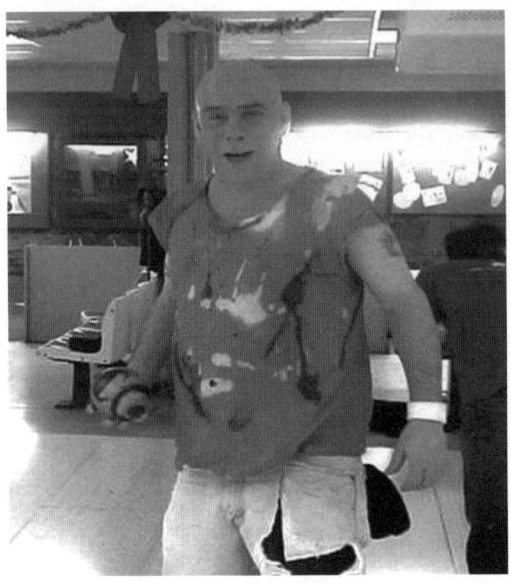

Newly crowned WCB champion Greg "Agamemnon" Lebelle.

trash, welfare case, illiterate, out-of-shape pissant try and defeat the most dangerous man in the history of 5-pin? This is my piece of fucking earth. This pine, right here, Towell. Ted, you see this, you piece of shit, this is my property. My lane. I own this. Do you know that? Because these people sure as hell know this. I am this world. This isn't about a 7-10 split, or rolling a turkey, or whatever. This is my hell, and you are in it. And I don't care what kind of accolades you bring, all your stupid promos and trophies and plastic endorsement deals with Burger King, you can't beat me, you won't beat me, you will never ever, walk again if you don't get off my goddamn lane right now. Towell, I appreciate the fact that you want to give the fans something to watch, but I'm not going to face this piece of crap ever! So Ted, I'm gonna give you the chance right now to save your stupid life, to let your kids still respect you, to let your wife still love you, to let your trainers and bowling friends still think you're one heck of a guy because son, if you sign that goddamn contract to fight me for the WCB title at GUTTERWARS, I will fuck

> "I NEVER SAW ANYONE CUT A PROMO BEFORE LIKE LEBELLE DID THAT NIGHT. IT WAS A LIVE HOUSE SHOW, TWO WEEKS BEFORE THE PAY-PER-VIEW, AND THAT TED GUY WAS SO SCARED, I REMEMBER JERRY TOMLIN JUST LAUGHING THAT WE HAD TO CHANGE THE CARD BECAUSE THE GUY WAS SO SPOOKED. HE TOTALLY WET HIS PANTS. HE NEVER SPOKE TO ANYONE FROM WCB EVER AGAIN."
> — JORDAN BINNER

you up and buffet your guts all over this alley. I will open up this lane, and put in your goddamn skull, to be found in the future by archeologists trying to unravel the facts about the legend that is Me! Now get the fuck out of my bowling alley."

It was Friday afternoon and traffic curbed the corner of the building in which Robert Towell paced. He combed his desk for a mint, past a tide of stamps and paperclips. He couldn't find it. This pissed him off. The building moved in tense rat-like hiccups. Elevators shafts vibrated the wrong way, coffee machines gurgled unplugged and photocopiers, seldom used for pornographic memorandums, overheated and flat-lined. He was nervous and excited, a bit preoccupied with the fall merchandising schedule. He was up to his nose in the usual bullshit.

"Yeah, three units of Lebelle T-shirts in two weeks. We'll do Wallmart, Zellers and one of the others I can't remember. The new line of action figures as well. Series III." He motioned to the other man in his office to take a seat. "Look I have a meeting now, gotta go. Talk to you when you're back from Chicago."

In front of Robert Towell sat Black Ninja Seven, Lebelle's opponent for the evening's pay-per-view, the first without former champion, and WCB poster-boy Dragan Momchilo on the card. "I've been speaking to Lebelle, he's very happy to be working with you this weekend," Robert tried to reassure the Ninja, who was not in his Ninja costume but wore a pair of blue corduroy pants and a grey sweatshirt with a hood.

"Okay, but when am I..."

"Look," Towell said, standing up to stretch his corporate legs, "Ninja baby, I want something to be clear. You are being paid to lose. This is a big match, we need to sell Lebelle as the champion."

"You said I would get a push."

"You are. You're getting some manufacturing and there are the very popular *Black Ninja School of Bowling* T-shirts that you and Black Ninja Six are both benefiting from. If you've noticed at each event there are more and more of those shirts in the crowds. I'm sure Linda in accounting has issued you, on more than one occasion, your royalty check?"

"Yes. But I thought I would start to actually win matches," Black Ninja Seven said.

"Maybe, maybe this will happen. But I want you to think about this, do you really want your first victory to be in, of all places, Ajax?"

"I'm not resigning at the end of the year."

"That's fine. We'll get someone else to wear your uniform anonymously. You can have it your way."

"I just want one big run on top."

"Don't we all."

A buzzer interrupted the tense office setting.

"Sir, Dragan Momchilo is on line one."

"Put him on, and it's not Sir Dragan Momchilo, why would he be knighted? For paranoia? Bad acting?"

There was a scuttle in the hallway, Robert saw Jerry Tomlin and Greg Lebelle coming into the frame of his office doorway.

"Put Dragan on hold."

"Yes sir," the receptionist said.

"Look," Robert said to Seven, "you don't see *me* trying to become WCB champion, running in and picking up a bowling ball, stealing the show. We're a team. And on this team, you lose."

"We're going to a signing with Godfrey, just came by to get some money for the day," Jerry said poking his nose into the office.

"What time are they expecting you guys? It's the toy store then the splash park today right?" Robert grinned efficiently. Jerry nodded.

"We get to go on the rides for free with a bunch of the kids from 2:00-5:00 PM. Or wait, no it's 2:30."

"Yep," Lebelle said, his face a bit pale.

"You feeling okay?"

"Yeah, tired."

"Get some tomato juice, or something with Vitamin C," Robert said, his voice genuinely concerned.

"Okay."

"Come on, get excited. You don't see Steve Yzerman getting to do this in Motown do you boys? Yes, this is good PR if I do say so. Make sure Brenda gives you some glossies for the autographs, and the new calendars too; I think there are some boxes of them in the lobby." Robert walked over to the window and looked down at the view, but remembering he was still on the phone, returned to the small holes in the mouth piece.

"Dragan, how's your game?"

"Look, I got an idea. For tonight, just trust me."

"I trust you. What's your idea?"

"Well, I want to come across as more aggressive, I was thinking about what you said."

"About you being a passive predictable consumer instead of an innovative icon?"

"Yeah. I'm coming back for a backstage run-in, to get revenge for my loss at BOWLBASH."

"Okay, sounds good."

"What's going on?" Black Ninja Seven said.

"It's Dragan, we're thinking of a new angle tonight."

"Does it involve me?"

"Heavily. Okay, so Dragan, sorry, we'll talk later this afternoon, I'll tell security you're coming. Okay, gotta go meet Nikola for dinner, we've got a welted trout reservation at Flashlight, see you later tonight. Any idea when you want to come back, full-time?"

"I'll have a better idea later this week."

"How's soccer?"

"Good, real good. There was another fight this week."

"Great. Okay, talk to you later."

"So what's the plan?" asked the Ninja.

WCB GUTTERWARS

Plaza Bowl & Amusement
Ajax, Ontario
August 22, 1997

Sandbagger: Bowler who keeps his average down purposely in order to receive a higher handicap than he deserves.

Sandwich game: A 200 game scored by alternating strikes and spares. (Dutch 200)

Scenic route: Path taken by a big curve ball.

Schleifer: Thin-hit strike where pins seem to fall one by one.

Robert Towell had chosen Ajax, Ontario for the location of GUTTERWARS for several reasons: it was "Hollywood" Dragan Momchilo's childhood town, and there were two rival bowling alleys on Harwood Avenue south. Towell loved the idea of a ratings war, no matter how brief. "It's great fun for me. Like watching two Mom and Pop shops staring at each other from across the street, crying over who is buying a pack of gum." But mainly, as Towell told a local radio station, Ajax was chosen because, "It's so damn exotic. Reasonably priced mini-golf parks, nice flower delivery shops as well. Our bowlers appreciate these two nuances, and therefore, Ajax gets the thumbs up."

The cameras rolled. The diminutive Dale Godfrey stood beside Black Ninja Seven in his dressing room wearing a second-hand blazer (wool and mustard colour) and his trademark toque. He butted out his cigarette with a garish smile and cleared his congested throat as best as he could. The Ninja was in his usual cotton ensemble.

The summer had been a hot one, and no amount of underground ventilation or dusty ceiling fans could change the mood of the evening. The audience sported their best collective vacant stare. "It was like Ninja soup," recalls Towell. "There were an especially high number of fans in Ninja-ware, and they were all sweating, standing in zombied silence."

Dale stood next to the challenger and began the interview that would be telecast after the Lebelle segment, which was going live: "Black Ninja Seven, you're up next against WCB champion Greg Lebelle. What's going through your head right now?"

"I just hope my kids aren't watching," Black Ninja Seven said, avoiding the camera's penetrating gaze.

"Why, because it's past their bedtime?"

"No," he said, looking nervously towards the camera. "I'm really itchy Jerry, can we cut this dumb interview?" Black Ninja Seven, truth be told, was more ashamed than the other bowlers. His kids preferred to pepper their room with posters of Greg Lebelle and Dragan Momchilo. They didn't even own their own father's bowling action figure.

In a vacant hallway, Jerry Tomlin stood beside the sweat ogre Greg "Agamemnon" Lebelle for the opening shot of GUTTERWARS. "I've been working out all afternoon," Lebelle boasted.

The crew and stars had spent the day with the locals, handing out flyers and some free tickets to fill out the cheaper seats in the back. Lebelle was at the gym, taking his role as champ seriously.

Tomlin was sweating beside the giant. A sleepless night in a local motel with a broken air conditioner, coupled with the new script changes at the last minute, had flustered the loyal employee.

"We're joined now live here in Ajax, Ontario by newly crowned WCB champion Greg 'Agamemnon' Lebelle. What are your plans for tonight's big title defense here at GUTTERWARS?"

Lebelle, sporting a worn leather jacket over his naked upper quarters snorted the underground air with panache. "Tonight's big title defense? I've got a guy in a pair of cotton pajamas. This is a cakewalk. And until the WCB board can get their act together and find me some decent com-

"Hollywood" Dragan Momchilo relaxes in his native town of Ajax, Ontario with a WCB fan.

petition, I'll tell you, this is the easiest job I've ever had."

"How do you feel about the five frame rule, as oppose to the traditional ten frames?"

"What about it? Jesus, what are you, a reporter or something? All that means is it'll take ten minutes to destroy his life instead of thirty."

Jerry Tomlin turned from the champion and faced the camera, adjusting his tie with some vaudeville flare. "A confident Lebelle is ready for his match-up tonight; let's go down to lane sixteen. Robert?"

"Folks, this is going to be a great day for pro bowling," Towell said with a sycophantic snarl. "Take a look at this crowd, they are really behind the Ninja tonight!"

The crowd swooned and cheered as the camera operators gobbled up their likenesses. Meanwhile, backstage, Greg "Agamemnon" Lebelle walked towards a catering table and picked up an apple from a bowl. A Ninja approached him and nodded.

"You ready for tonight?"

The Ninja nodded. As Lebelle turned his head and continued on his casual stroll, the Ninja hit the champion on the side of the head with a fire extinguisher.

Lebelle muttered, on his knees, temporarily dazed. The cameraman, who had been filming from a few feet back, rushed to the fallen Lebelle. The play-by-play cued in, the pay-per-view was underway for the paying home audience. At the WCB desk, Towell dashed into the narrative spread.

"I can't tell for sure, but it seems like, wait, yes, Lebelle has been laid out by Black Ninja Seven."

Lebelle moaned slightly, rolling onto his stomach, clenching his skull. *Once I had a dream, I left everything I cherished to cleanse myself, to cease, to feel like an object. I took a final look back at what I was leaving and the only thing that hurt to leave for good was you Richard...*

"Looks like Black Ninja Seven has struck early and first," said Dale Godfrey.

"I don't think Lebelle saw it coming," Robert Towell told the crowd and the folks at home. The camera tried to follow the Ninja as he ran out the back door of the building, fire extinguisher in hand.

"It looks like he's high-tailed it out of the building," noted Godfrey, clutching the rim of his toque.

Robert Towell adjusted himself in his chair. He and Dale Godfrey were joined by Jordan Binner, who had a big smile on his face.

"Folks tonight's main event is brought to you by Harold's Meat and I am joined by Jordan Binner, how are things Jordan?"

"Things are fantastic, I'm training down in the minor leagues and hope to be back from my injury in a few weeks."

"That's good news for your fans, and what do you think about our main event, which is next?"

"Well Rob, I think that the moment still lies with Lebelle, he's bigger and this should be no trouble for the champ," Jordan Binner said.

"I can't believe that attack," Dale Godfrey said.

"You've gotta wonder though, despite his confidence, that somewhere down the road Lebelle will have to face Dragan Momchilo again."

"Well yeah, I mean Dragan was royally screwed at BOWLBASH, we all saw what went down."

"As we wait to get some medical attention to the champion, let's take a look at the footage from that controversial finish."

A brief chorus of boos followed the clip. *No rest,* Towell thought, watching the monitor and caressing his walkie-talkie. "Okay, follow him," he ordered the crew.

Backstage, locked in a frenzy of groggy anger, Lebelle began to scour the area for the Ninja who had attacked him. In his taped-up hand was the gaudy WCB championship trophy. A crew member found Black Ninja Six and Seven talking and rushed Seven away.

"Lebelle is pissed from your cheap shot, better go start the match," the official said, pushing the Ninja out into the main hallway leading to the bowling alley.

"What cheap shot?" said Black Ninja Seven, rubbing dry skin cream into his face.

As medics tried to gage Lebelle's state, the champion pushed them aside. "Fuck off, I'm fine," he said, with his eyes locked on lane sixteen. When he passed the WCB broadcast desk, he grabbed a spare microphone, and nodded. Red wire trickles of blood weaseled down his face.

"Hey Rob," Lebelle shouted with a giant sneer. "This one's going be a snap, gonna take a lot more than a cheap shot to get rid of me. Come on Ninja Twelve," Lebelle snorted sarcastically, spitting the blood that had consolidated into the folds of his lips. He growled into the microphone, and tossed it back on the desk.

Deep in the nose bleeder seats, behind a predictable billow of cigarette smoke "Hollywood" Dragan Momchilo sat, creepy-eyed, burning Lebelle's image into his eyes. He dug his soccer cleats into the concrete floor below him.

From the backstage area, Black Ninja Seven entered and made his way towards lane sixteen.

"Here comes Black Ninja Seven, what was he thinking attacking Lebelle like that?" Towell said, playing up the angle. "I wouldn't want to be in his shoes, and I'm not talking foot odour."

"What is Lebelle going to do to him? I mean, we saw what happened backstage, it seems like Black Ninja Seven was really trying to put the champ out of commission," Jerry Tomlin added, to fuel the controversy.

Seeing his attacker at the lip of conflict, Lebelle put down the WCB championship trophy and began to charge the Ninja with rhino like quickness and determination. Only the speed of a WCB crew person could capture the beast on film, and that he did, with instant replay to back up the unconverted. Lebelle grabbed the Ninja by the throat, picked him up and put him over his head and began the short walk back to lane sixteen.

"Oh man, I would not want to be the Ninja right now. I'm guessing he wished he hadn't clocked Lebelle," Dale Godfrey said, so excited he began a small coughing fit that kept him out of play-by-play until the next frame.

Greg Lebelle took the Ninja halfway down the lane and threw him into the pins, getting a strike. Picking up the Ninja for a second throw, Lebelle waited for the pins to reset. "The referee is indicating it's now the Ninja's turn, but Lebelle could care less, and shrugs off the instruction!" Lebelle tossed the Ninja head-first into the pins, repeating the Ninja strike and laughed sickly on his way back to the foul line.

"The beast has awoken in our WCB champion," Jerry Tomlin exploded. "The game is tied, and not a single ball has been thrown!"

At the end of the fourth frame Lebelle gave up on the Ninja-as-ball routine and threw him into lane fourteen.

"Lebelle is finishing this game the old fashioned way," Robert Towell proclaimed.

"It's about time, I couldn't stand watching that anymore," Dale Godfrey said from the comfort of his chair.

The cameras scanned the live audience. Sitting with two soccer players in the crowd, Momchilo was feeling sad and mean; he was not wearing that habitual smile. He looked fucked up, a bit raw, a bit ruined, like a scalded dog, wondering when its limbs would heal from the untraceable laceration. The smoke made his blue eyes sink deeper into his thin face, his head appeared to be shrinking, his skin, deeply tanned from days above the surface of the bowling alley, out on the soccer field, needed sleep, demanded it, but he stayed awake, and watched the event. The smell of cola refreshed his anger and made his eyelids heavy. He got up and walked out of the building as the WCB logo sprung up, concluding the pay-per-view.

He punched the air in front of him, bumping into a doughy fan on the way out of the building. He loved the competition, he cared for it, and he missed it. But Dragan knew the best part of the night was just ahead. He lit a cigarette and began to change into the Ninja-wear from a stashed bag in the back lot. Dragan knew he would be back, and back on top within a month, but in the meantime, he had to show Lebelle who was really running the show, at least for tonight.

"Here is your winner, and still undisputed WCB champion, Greg Lebelle."

Black Ninja Six went to the aid of her comrade Seven.

At the entrance stood a third Black Ninja holding a fire extinguisher.

"Hey Lebelle," the Ninja mocked into a mic, slowly removing the mask. "I haven't forgotten who you are. I know who you are. I know everything about you. And I'm going to take back what's mine. Just so you know I'm serious, I have a little tailoring job I'm doing for you, a favour if you will." The crowd ignited in cheers, realizing the Ninja was in fact Dragan Momchilo.

A stunned Lebelle stood jaw locked, his neck slowly turned towards Towell who was smiling. Dragan Momchilo pulled out Greg Lebelle's leather jacket and lit a cig-

BLACK NINJA SEVEN WAS THE SECOND NINJA WHO WORE BLACK FOR THE COMPANY. WHY DID YOU GET SUCH A BIG PUSH AND WHY DO YOU THINK THE NINJA PHENOMENON, OR LACK THEREOF, WAS SO POORLY SOLD?

Dragan: He wanted it too bad. We (Greg and I) told him to find his inner voice, maybe a new gimmick? But Black Ninja Seven? I mean come on, we couldn't stop laughing when he was around. The both of them. I felt sorry for his kids.

Greg: Black Ninja Six and Seven were ignored simply because NO ONE LIKES SEQUELS! They were unoriginal, heck, look at their names.

Robert: For Christmas one year I got both of the Ninjas matching nightcaps, though not on purpose. I believe there were little stars on the tops of the hats. I gave them their gifts separately, about three hours apart. I guess I could have planned out their characters a bit more, but basically, I needed some steady losers to fit the roster, and they seemed willing to play along. I mean it was their job right?

arette. He took a few drags, and tossed the lit cigarette on the leather, setting it ablaze. Holding the fire extinguisher mockingly, then shaking his head side to side, he sneered at the champion, dropping the fire extinguisher and leaving the coat to burn as WCB programming and copyright credits rolled up on the screen.

"This has been a pivotal night here at WCB, a pivotal night, we'll keep you posted, we'll see you next time!" Jerry Tomlin, wrapped up the new swerve as the crowd's rolling applause sealed the program.

ROBERT & NIKOLA TOWELL'S APARTMENT

TORONTO, ONTARIO
MARCH 7, 1998

The elevator tried hard to keep him calm, but Robert Towell was up to his eyelashes in stress, after pulling a series of all-nighters.

He tried to be objective on his cellphone, "Forget *Ghostbusters II* or *Episode II*, even *Annie II,* this is the sequel that counts. I mean, how can we keep putting another Roman numeral after the brand name event? It's so Superbowl." That was Towell, three hours before the final dress rehearsal of BOWLBRAWL II. At the other end of the line, on the emergency WCB hotline, Jerry Tomlin assured his boss that all would be well.

"All will be well."

"Some nights, you know, I feel like I've tofued my way through life long enough, and no matter how trendy a guy I am, I just can't make bowling any better or worse than it already is, and I just want to gut all my employees and dry them out on a polluted beach."

"I understand Rob," Tomlin said, unable to think of anything else to say.

"I'll see you backstage at seven," Towell said and hung up the phone, entered his apartment, and began the ritual of undress. His bath awaited his grand entrance. "I love these automated bathing systems, glad I had them installed. As well, I'm glad I installed these voice activated vanity recording systems, in case I get amnesia, and want to be nostalgic."

For Robert Towell, the day started with grey milkshakes splashing against his inner jaw. Somehow the food had to get down, to make him live again, past this concrete week that had scalded him in fluorescent office lighting for the better part of 140 hours. Towell himself was not a skin shade but could only be described in Watts. He slipped into the bath and came up.

"I feel like I'm at about the 32 Watt level now," he'd tell Nikola when she asked how he was feeling. She had returned home, moments after "operation bath" had begun.

"Do I look sexy?" she asked from the balcony, in a muted gray mini and backless fuchia top.

"Don't worry, your sales meeting will go fine."

"Thanks, I just want to know, because you're always honest with me about it," Nikola said. She packed a back-up ensemble (transparent chiffon Miyake shirt, Dolce bra, and skin tight empire waist secretary skirt) and grabbed a file from her bedroom dresser, one she'd prayed was there. And it was, untouched and unburglarized.

"Yes, you look beautiful, powerful, and sexy."

"Thanks Rob. You'll pick me up before the event tonight?"

"Yes. I'll pick you up in the lobby downstairs."

As she left she kissed him and squeezed his bum under the bath. The couple were always in flight.

As he dressed, Robert reworked some of the script for the evening to include the news that Dale Godfrey had become interim president while Robert Towell was on holidays. It was the board's idea; apparently, the fans had been reacting to Towell's bossy heel character, and thought if there was to be isolated conflict at the top of the bowling hierarchy, it should be between Lebelle and Momchilo, and Godfrey's neutrality and non-threatening appearance as administrative boss would compliment this concept. Robert Towell's on-camera appearances were very controversial; since most smart fans knew he ran things backstage, they didn't need to be reminded of it constantly at live events.

Jordan Binner was not even considered for the prestigious role because of his age and his inexperience, but the fans seemed to enjoy Dale Godfrey's appearance, and even with a toque on, the board believed he would "appeal to the common man."

In between bites of tofu burritos in his study, Towell dialled up Jerry again, his constant ear-slave. "This is crap, but it'll work," he said over the phone.

"Just go with it, I think it'll work, and just think, you have the night off," Jerry told Robert.

"I never have the night off. When I was on camera it seemed I had more breathing room," Robert said, clicking the *send* button to the script prompt manager.

WCB BOWLBRAWL II

O'CONNOR BOWL
EAST YORK, ONTARIO
MARCH 7, 1998

SQUEEZE: The action of the second and third fingers against the thumb, much like snapping the fingers, as they deliver the ball.

STEAL: To get more pins than you deserve on a strike hit.

STIFF / STIFF ALLEY: A lane with a tendency to hold a hook ball back.

SPARE: All pins down with two balls.

SPLASHER: A strike where the pins are downed quickly.

SPLIT: A spare leave in which the headpin is down and the remaining combination of pins have an intermediate pin down immediately ahead of or between them.

SPOT BOWLING: Target on lane at which the bowler aims; could be a dot, a board, or an arrow.

WCB NOTES

WCB.COM has announced the ticket prices for Bowlbrawl II. Laneside seats will be $750, including a chair you get to take home. Other seats will be $200, $100, $75, $50, and $40. Ticket prices are down slightly from last year.

The crowd of bowling fanatics that Towell had manufactured hissed like vipers unfed for weeks. Their tongues flicked fillings and began to burrow deep into saliva tombs with the sound of teeth dissolving in sugar. Many fans wore the freshly silkscreened *BOWLBRAWL II: I'M IN THE SEQUEL* T-shirt.

In the belly of O'Connor Bowl paced a smoking "Hollywood" Dragan Momchilo, the man who was billed by WCB promo writers as "the only natural athlete in the history of WCB." As Dragan moved back and forth in front of the camera, his soccer team filed in around him. Some were larger, older, some were smaller, but they all wore their green and white outfits and they were all hypnotized by the spectacle.

"You work here?"

"Sometimes."

There was a group nod and as Momchilo continued to smoke, the floor director approached the group and got the make-up artist to touch up some of the rougher members of the team.

"You've all signed the waivers, you are not to talk during the live interviews, and we've cleared your team's logo with our sponsors and networks, that is all fine, so just relax, look tough, support Dragan during this spot and you know what happens at the end, so just wait for your cues." The director disappeared down a hallway with a scurry of assistants and clipboards.

"Is this for real?" one asked.

"Is what for real? He's our soccer team captain. I just want to hang out with him. It's better than hanging out with my parents."

"Is this how he trains?" said another player.

"What are we doing here? This is sort of lame."

As he walked down the low-lit hallway Jerry Tomlin finished his tuna and avocado sandwich with a lot of joy. He ripped off his paper bib, and extended a clean hand as he approached the soccer players.

"How's it going?"

"Pretty good."

"You ready for tonight?" Tomlin asked, his gross tongue detecting a bit of heavy avocado on the side of his mouth.

"Yep, I think so. I think I've, I mean, we've got the finish down pat." Momchilo said, nodding to his teammates.

"I have some money riding on this match, any chance you're going to win by 10 points?" Jerry Tomlin said in a hush.

"I can't tell you that. Rob told me about your problem too, so don't think I haven't been warned."

"Okay, let's go." As the camera rolled, Jerry introduced the event, his location and why he was in the basement of a bowling alley alone. Momchilo walked into the frame and smiled. One by one his team surrounded him.

"Dragan can we ask you a few questions before your big match?"

The rest of his teammates poured in around him, filling up the shot. Jerry Tomlin looked slightly nervous as the team members finned into the frame from the hallway.

"Okay. Why don't you ask what I am doing here with Greg Lebelle? The main event, the sequel, BOWLBRAWL II, the biggest night in this business. Why the hell do I bother with this company when I have a real sport to fall back on?"

The soccer players began to laugh and smear grins into the camera. Momchilo grabbed the microphone from Tomlin and the camera zoomed in tight along his stubbled face. This was no youth, this was a man charged in the ever growing balm of machismo in which he had been destined to cameo. His confidence was enhanced by the soccer team's glow – and Momchilo knew, he knew they had his back tonight, even if they had no idea of the consequence, the meaning, they were there for him.

Momchilo flared at the mic: "Greg, you fucking idiot, this is all you have. All you have is that trophy and a pathetic sport by the jugular. Big deal. Tonight I'm going to show you I'm bigger than this whole building, the telecast, all the merchandising and gambling and colour commentators combined. Did you read those cheat sheets? I'm favoured tonight, I'm gonna make a whole shitload of strangers rich tonight. Tonight, I'm going to show my grandmother that I didn't steal the sugar, and I'm going to show my father that it *was* my fate. Well tonight, with my soccer team, I'm going to right a wrong. You see Lebelle, Towell screwed me out of the WCB title, but it wasn't like I cared. But I know you live in a world that is psychedelic, unhinged and full of pain. I know who you are and what makes you sad. This ends tonight."

"Well you heard it from the challenger, he's ready and we're going now to lane sixteen for an important update."

They cut to a promo and prepared for the next shot, lane-side.

"What?" Momchilo asked.

"Rob says that's enough, I have my orders," Jerry Tomlin said, sighing out a wave of relief.

"Gimme that," Momchilo said, taking the cellphone from Jerry's blazer pocket. "Towell, it's me. Just a minute guys," he said, nodding to his team.

"Dragan, nice work," Towell said from his car, watching on his personal monitor. As he drove he steadily peeled back a layer of skin from a fresh pineapple while separating a pomegranate in half to reveal the juicy red seed orgy that would soon dissolve in the lips of both him and his wife.

"I don't know Rob, that didn't sound so good, I thought I should have ended with: I know you have deep seeded philosophical relationships with your status as a bowling god. You've crippled yourself with mythology. But tonight, I'm going to take back the title, tonight I'm going to show you that I am the only real athlete ever to play professional bowling, and that I am the master of all that is round, and what are you going to do Lebelle when the true champion leaves BOWLBRAWL II the undisputed champion? I'm not 83 years old Lebelle. This isn't some promo high school drama sketch with me in drag playing my grandmother. This is the real fucking…"

"No, Dragan it was fine. Calm down, I'll see you soon."

Sitting down in front of lane sixteen at the WCB broadcast desk Jerry Tomlin and Dale Godfrey, the acting president of WCB, stood with headsets ready, waiting for the guest referee to be announced. Godfrey ate some popcorn while Jerry waved to some local fans that were holding signs.

"Folks, if this is anything like its predecessor, BOWLBRAWL II will be a slobber knocker of a sequel, a hell of a pay-per-view and the best damn main event in the history of professional sports. Momchilo versus Lebelle, and it's up next!"

Backstage Jordan Binner filled in for Tomlin's usual interview spot. He wore a powder-blue tuxedo that was really tight and he hoped it didn't appear too obvious that it was cutting off circulation in his ribs.

"Lebelle, you've been champion now for a few months and during this time you've been praised as the biggest star in the history of WCB. But can you confirm these allegations by some staff members that you viciously assaulted your opponent's grandmother last week at a grocery store?"

"No. I can't. I mean, we've seen that footage from a year ago right, I have had absolutely no contact with Dragan's grandmother. I have nothing further on this subject to offer you. I can't do anything for you because you are not my opponent. The only thing I am going to do for anyone tonight is show them that I cannot be beat by a single man, or his grandmother." Lebelle walked out of the frame with his championship trophy clasped tightly in his hand.

The match began with the larger Lebelle dominating the scrawny youth. By the third frame it seemed as if no bowling at all was taking place, Dale Godfrey was screaming at both men to actually throw balls down the ramp.

Jerry Tomlin covered for Godfrey who tried to appease both the fans and the two competitors.

"Dale Godfrey, the president of WCB, is screaming at both men to compete. There have been a series of gutters thrown for nearly five frames here folks, with the score tied at 16."

"I'm not letting you win this Dragan," Lebelle said, his hands around Momchilo's arm, an arm that reached for a ball from the ball return.

"I'm not leaving here tonight without your title." Momchilo countered with a cheap trick assisted by Jerry Tomlin, who had handed him a small box of thumbtacks earlier in the evening.

"Oh my, Momchilo has just dumped a pile of tacks all over that bowling alley, and is egging Lebelle to charge him," Jerry Tomlin told the vast crowd.

As Lebelle charged the challenger, Momchilo ascended into the air, landing on the ball return. He followed this defensive by jumping onto Lebelle's back, forcing the champion to land face first on the tacks.

"Oh my God! This is insane!" Tomlin cried.

The challenger followed up with a series of kicks in the gut, sending Lebelle and some of his blood to crawl off to the side. Momchilo worked the crowd. He grabbed a 10-pin ball and threw it down the 5-pin lane, getting a strike.

"That's a strike," Tomlin shouted.

As the fourth frame chimed in on the small score screen, which was being projected live onto the WCB website in a slicker format, both men made their way to the lip of the pins and looked at Godfrey for the answer.

"Who's turn is it?" Lebelle said, with a strangling grip around Momchilo's neck.

"I don't know."

"I want to know whose pins I'm kicking down."

"Yeah, that's important to know," Momchilo said, strangling Lebelle back.

"I'm not leaving my post here to find out."

"Me neither."

Godfrey clued in and stood up from the booth, he pointed at the screen and then to Momchilo. He indicated with his left hand that it was the fifth and final frame. "It's your turn," he mouthed to Momchilo.

Sensing victory, Lebelle tossed Momchilo into the lane adjacent to the combat and ran towards the ball return where he began to throw gutters. This would keep Momchilo's score the same, while he could accumulate more in the final frame.

Momchilo bolted up from the crumpled position in which he had landed and waved to his soccer team for the save. On cue three balls made their way down the lane, and within the time of Lebelle's first gutter, Momchilo had knocked down all the pins.

"The tie has just been broken, thanks in part to Momchilo's soccer team!" Tomlin declared. "It's now Lebelle's turn, this is his only chance to catch up and retain the title."

An enraged Greg Lebelle threw one ball into Momchilo's guts, knocking him to the ground. Another hand clobbered an enthusiastic soccer teammate.

Lebelle stood at the edge of the lane, Momchilo's fallen corpse lay demented in front of the pins, trying to protect his lead by not allowing the pins to get knocked down. At this stage of the match, it was his only chance at regaining the championship.

Greg Lebelle puffed on a half-spent cigarette and took his trophy from the broadcast desk and began to stalk Momchilo, who was making his way towards the champion with his fists above his face, protecting him-

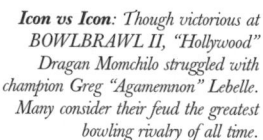

Icon vs Icon*: Though victorious at BOWLBRAWL II, "Hollywood" Dragan Momchilo struggled with champion Greg "Agamemnon" Lebelle. Many consider their feud the greatest bowling rivalry of all time.*

self. Gaining speed, Lebelle had Momchilo lined up, and was about to finish off the challenger when Momchilo ducked to avoid the champ's trophy swing. "Fucking psycho!"

With adrenaline back in his system, Momchilo sprinted to the ball return, while Lebelle ran towards the erect pins. It was a matter of time, and the crowd sensed the immediacy to their dilemma; could Lebelle knock down the pins in time, or could Momchilo throw three gutter balls, end the frame and match to solidify the victory?

The first ball hit Lebelle in the back of the leg, sending him crashing to the ground. But the computer didn't register the ball's movement as part of the frame. A gale of stale cheers stung both competitors. "He landed funny," someone said to their friend.

"Lebelle's lip is cut," Jerry Tomlin said. "This is getting ugly, and it's getting ugly fast."

Lebelle picked up the ball in his hands and pointed to the remaining pins.

"Hollywood" Dragan Momchilo sent the second and third balls into the gutter until there was one left, one ball to determine the match.

Lebelle stood four feet from the pins with a demonic grin on his face. His skull was sweating under the lights, and he was favouring his left side.

"It looks like Lebelle is going to... oh my!"

"That's horrific!" Tomlin cried. Lebelle hit the ground as the crowd caught their breath. "With the precision of an archer, a member of Team Momchilo has landed a soccer cleat into the back of Lebelle's head."

"And the champ is not moving!"

"This shows how far Momchilo will go to regain the championship!"

As Lebelle carefully reached behind to pull the cleat from his head, Momchilo rolled the final gutter in between the champion's unstable legs.

Lebelle, exhausted, outplayed and derailed, clenched his eyes in disappointment.

The announcer seared the audience with the verdict: "Here is your winner, by a score of 67-64, and once again WCB champion, 'Hollywood' Dragan Momchilo!"

After several hours at payphones "freaking out beyond his years," Towell recalls, "Hollywood" Dragan Momchilo finally got through to Robert Towell who was touring around in his car with Katherine Cockshutt, going over some numbers and proofs.

"Okay, so Victoria Terrace, toy store, look for the crying Serbian chain-smoker," Robert Towell barked with torpedo precision.

Thanks to Robert's latest obsession of eating seafood in the dark, they were on their way to meet Nikola at Flashlight, a new restaurant that, in addition to being completely devoid of light, boasted an endless audio of soothing new age Moroccan world music (and of course flashlights as part of the utensils). It was teeming with the freshest P.E.I. potatoes and mussels, not to mention welted trout, which was actually a faux-trout made of tofu, spinach, and sticky rice.

He told Katherine to be patient, claiming it was a minor emergency. "Ten minutes tops, I'll talk to him, then we'll eat. Jesus, it's like a crisis centre sometimes, like the guy is hanging on the side of an asteroid screaming for his life."

Outside of Toys R Us it was a typical cold early Spring morning where "Hollywood" Dragan Momchilo paced and twitched alone across from a dive coffee joint which was, according to Towell's criticism, a place to drink "clown coffee". Momchilo took his coffee with three creams and three sugars, a marvel to the circulation system of any athlete. Momchilo seemed bent on creating an antidote for the fast food athlete stigma that has been plaguing North American obesity clinics and sport-obsessed fatties for years. Momchilo was rack-thin, but ate like a slutty diabetic, one who had crawled over the electronic fence of a rehabilitation centre on a nightly basis.

Robert Towell's car pulled up to the curb and a window rolled down.

"Dragan, how are you? You remember Katherine, the photographer? Anyway, let's talk, hold on Katherine."

Robert Towell exited the car and nodded back to Katherine who was on her cellphone and was flipping through the proofs of the latest WCB program in which her photography appeared.

"How's it going?" Momchilo said.

"You asked me to meet you," Robert Towell replied, shaking the young

WHEN YOU STARTED HAVING UNCONTROLLABLE ALIEN RAPE NIGHTMARES, YOU SPOKE TO TOWELL ABOUT THEM. IT BECAME PART OF THE MARKETING PLOY, TOWELL EVEN HAD YOU DOING CONDOM COMMERCIALS WITH "ALIEN" GIRLS IN LINGERIE, THEIR SKIN ALL PAINTED IN GREEN AND BLUE SCALES. EVERYTHING SEEMED HUMOUROUS, BUT QUITE DARK. WAS IT LIKE THE PLANT WITH SHADE AND THE PLANT WITHOUT SHADE ANALOGY, YOU GET DARKNESS FROM DARKNESS? LESS GROWTH WITHOUT LIGHT? I MEAN IF YOU GUYS WERE PLAYING BASEBALL IN THE SUN YOU PROBABLY WOULDN'T HAVE BEEN SO DEPRESSED?

Dragan: Yeah, telling Towell anything was a nightmare in itself. I think he used it to control me. It's a weird form of psychology, but Towell would tell me he could make the nightmares go away. For awhile they did, but they really fucked me up.

WERE YOU AND GREG LEBELLE GROWING APART OR GETTING CLOSER AS WCB'S AUDIENCE SWELLED?

Dragan: It was off and on, I would crash on his couch sometimes, when we were working on certain characterizations of our stories. One night I was really fucked up about this girl and I was crying. He lit candles for me and told me to cry, that it was okay. Later that night he woke up, and told me he had this dream where he was chasing his brother Richard. He was running behind him and finally caught him. But when he turned him around it was me. That freaked me out. We were close, but it was always strange.

man's hand and pointing to a nearby stretch of sidewalk. He knew it would have to be outdoors, as most of the toy stores and shops on the strip were non-smoking environments, unlike Momchilo's life. But what did Towell care? The tobacco companies still paid their advertising dues, and were even considering advertising on some of the merchandise packaging. It was a fine way to spend your money, Towell thought, watching Momchilo light another cigarette. It was popular, and that was all that mattered.

"So what's up?" Momchilo asked nervously.

"No, you don't understand, I was invited here, you can't say what is up to me. Just tell me what your problem is now; you always have some problem with something. Otherwise I wouldn't hear from you," Robert said with a smile that doubled as an axe. He had sharp lips, properly balmed lips.

"I'm having these fucked up dreams Rob, all the time. I think it's these girls I meet on the road. I go out with them, hang out with them sometimes, but then I have nightmares. I'm afraid to answer my phone."

Robert smiled evilly, and began to speak, as if reading from lecture notes. "You're repressed. You're also self-indulgent, and you have serious emotional problems. When the editors and I watch the footage you always looked fucked up in every take, like you've just murdered someone and are waiting for the cops to break in the door."

"Do I?" Momchilo said, hissing as he inhaled.

"I'm afraid so. I think it's a permanent part of your disposition. That's why I wrote that ending with the net and sledgehammer last year. People would believe your disposition, based on body language alone. You look victimized most of the time, so it would only be natural that as the hero, you would overcome this, and have the crowd behind you. You seem to be suffering all the time."

"These dreams are fucked up. I'm at this party and these alien girls take me into this room and force me to have sex with them, and then drip green acid from their mouths on my stomach. Sometimes the girls are green, and speak in fucked up shrieks. Sometimes they have gills."

"That's interesting." For privacy's sake, Robert turned his face from Momchilo and pulled out his cellphone. He adjusted his coat according to various and obviously imaginary military naval routines.

"Michelle Winters? Listen, Robert Towell here, I've changed my mind on the condom campaign, and will get you some storyboards, maybe even a mock-up of the commercial I want to do for you, in like two days. Sound good? Get back to me or Jerry on Monday."

Momchilo smoked and watched Towell operate. He looked at the car behind him, pushing exhaust from the tailpipe. Robert re-directed his

WHAT WAS YOUR FIRST IMPRESSION OF THE BOWLING ENVIRONMENT AT THE HANDS OF ROBERT TOWELL AND WCB?

Dragan: They told me it was unscripted in the beginning. I trusted them. Until I found Robert Towell's blue folder. Dating back to early childhood, it had everything from my first doughnut to Lebelle's first beating stick. They used our histories to twist storylines and turn us into bowling assassins.

HOW DID YOUR FAMILY REACT TO YOUR CAREER MOVE INTO THE BOWLING ARTS?

Dragan: I was in the middle of a house show in Ajax I think, about three weeks into my contract, and I looked out into the crowd and saw my grandmother! And then Nick my brother! Robert had invited my entire family to the event. I had nightmares that their last memory of me before being swallowed up in sand or whatever Towell had planned for the audience, was me kicking this innocent bowler's head in for no apparent reason. In my nightmares I'd look over and my family would be on fire or whatever, Towell would be laughing. It was a lot of unnecessary stress. I never wanted my family to see that side of my life. Towell made sure they did.

attention to the doomed youth, who was creasing his face into three even face-folds.

"Aren't you going to help me?" Dragan Momchilo asked with a

slightly higher pitch, as if preparing to receive a serious self-inflicted burn by a kettle.

"You're going to help yourself. Do you know that one of the leading condom companies in the country wanted to sponsor us but I turned them down because I couldn't figure out how to use them, but now," Robert smiled and squeezed Momchilo's shoulder, "now, I know. Think of this: A giant poster, two hot alien sluts beside you, and you in the middle, holding a box of condoms, then the slogan, FOR EVERY SITUATION, CHOOSE VIKING CONDOMS."

"But how is that going to help me?"

"You'll see the girls on the set of the commercials, realize they are just actors, and maybe this will transfer into your subconscious. Also, we'll market some new Momchilo action figures; they'll come with your nightmares, some alien chicks, and we can put some condoms in those as well."

"What?"

"For a limited time. Okay, so, you've read the plans for BOWLBASH II, right, it's next month? I'll have Jerry call you for the commercial spots next week. Call me if you need anything."

Robert returned to the running car, Katherine waved from inside the vehicle, and soon, once again, Dragan Momchilo paced alone at the strip mall, unable to process the entirety of what had just transpired.

MALVERN HIGH SCHOOL

EAST YORK, ONTARIO
APRIL 9, 1998

INT. Front seat of Jerry's car. Jerry looks over to his right and watches Robert assemble gadgets, binoculars and walkie-talkies. Robert hands Jerry a headset.

EXT. Low-lit soccer field, 8:30 PM.

EXT. Shot of car parked across from soccer field.

INT. Dressed in dark ninja clothing Robert Towell and Jerry Tomlin sneak across the street to the soccer field.

Jerry:

What's the plan? What are we looking for?

Robert hands Jerry a small camera.

Robert:

Let's see if he's really playing soccer on top of his bowl-ing obligations. I want to know, I've invested a lot.

INT. Across the street Momchilo exits a car with two soccer players.

Jerry:

Is that him?

Robert: (sweating)

I'm going in for a closer look. You stay here, watch my back.

Jerry:

Okay.

Robert presses his back against the wall of the alley adjacent to the soccer field and creeps slowly behind the stands which surround the field. He snaps pictures sporadically.

Robert: (into walkie-talkie)

It's him alright. We better play this safe, I don't want to scare him off, we'll keep things the way they are, I just don't want him to leave us for soccer, it would look bad. See you back at the car.

Dragan Momchilo in action. Photo courtesy WCB surveillance.

Icons of NIK's evolution: *Backstage prep work at an early design meeting (circa 1996); stocking line photoshoot for catalogue (circa 1997); NIK's Spring launch (circa 1999); and the Viking/NIK fundraiser (circa 2000).*

ROBERT & NIKOLA TOWELL'S APARTMENT

Toronto, Ontario
April 19, 1998

"Yeah things are great, and we've got confirmation with this hot new designer, she's great," Nikola Towell said with a big gooey smile.

"Tons of lipgloss you dirty whore," Robert Towell said to his wife. "Tons. A cement truck full."

"Quit projecting, especially in front of company."

"Sorry didn't notice, got a lot of work to do, so whatever you girls do, do it without me."

"Oh Rob, lighten up," Katherine Cockshutt interjected, sharing the last slice of pizza with Martina.

Flooded with the scent of lipgloss and ass, perfume and sugar, the living room was operating like a well-lit theatre of the feminine persuasion. Nikola Towell and her leggy assistants pranced around in oversized African scarves and skirts, unfolded the pizza box and flipping through the new season's NIK catalogue, virtually ignored by Robert Towell, who sat on the sofa surrounded by bowling journals and the wall of his briefcase. He was knee deep in the Viking condom campaign, statistics, briefcase open, files everywhere. He didn't look up.

"Hey Robbie, the girls and I just got our prototypes back, so we're going to do a little fashion show here okay?"

"Yeah. Fine," Robert said, milling through a spreadsheet. "How are things pop tart?"

"Oh shut up Rob," Martina said playfully.

Robert returned to his work, "Glad we had this chat Martina, very productive."

"Okay girls," Nikola interjected, "let's try these things out."

Nikola began to unpack her Spring prototypes, scorched silk velvet scarves, tiny jewelled tie-around skirts, and weathered backless tops.

Robert Towell, oblivious to the bevy of half-naked women in the apartment, drenched himself in paperwork. He only saw two things: bowling and Nikola. Perhaps for Nikola it was a test, to see if he would sprout lecherous testicular fangs. But she was also knee deep in enterprise.

ROLLSCOURT TV PRODUCTION STUDIO

NORTH YORK, ONTARIO
APRIL 29, 1998

"Are you ready?" Jerry Tomlin asked the nervous Dragan Momchilo. Momchilo was silent, listening to the female voices as they grew louder. "Dragan, you ready?"

"Yeah, just a bit nervous."

"Relax. It's just a thirty second spot."

"Sorry, yeah, I guess so. I just got the script this morning," he said, sipping his large, three sugar, three cream coffee.

Momchilo and Jerry landed in a large studio area with a domestic set. In one of the two small make-up areas, two girls in bikinis were getting painted in green with some minor scales for, as Robert Towell called it: "That fresh for the prom, foreign slut look."

Momchilo was prepped in an adjacent, but separate, make-up area. Jerry Tomlin weaseled between the two make-up areas and went over any last minute script questions with the girls and Momchilo before sitting next to the director off-camera. "I bet you have a hairy back," one assistant said to him.

The actors were walked onto the kitchen set, and shown the bathroom where the additional shower scene would be shot.

"Okay, so you take a shower, the girls come in, you've read the script right?"

"Yep, all set."

INT. Close up.

Dragan's hair is wet, water is running. In his hand is soap.

Dragan:
(eyes closed)
Hello?

Girl's voice:
Hi boy. Are you almost done?

Dragan:
Who's there?

Second girl's voice:
Do you need a hand?

Dragan:
What's going on? How did you get into my house?

INT. Green alien hands pull curtain. Dragan's face in shock. Curtain is pulled to reveal two hot alien girls holding a towel.

INT. Two shot of alien girls smiling.

INT. Surrendering shot of Dragan, bemused.

INT. Dragan and two girls on couch.

Dragan:
Viking. Great for any, and I mean *any* situation.

Female alien voice over:
VIKING... Because you never know who's coming.
Or when....

INT. Camera operators nod, take off headsets, floor director exhales, director nods.

Director:
That was great everybody, we did it in one take, thanks.
Joni's got some forms for you to fill out.

Dragan:
That was cool. So you guys do a lot of commercials?

Alien #1:
(really pretentious, flipping cellphone,
sipping from water bottle)
Fuck no. Just doing Nik a favour. Come on Jenny let's go,
I want to get out of here. Nice to meet you Dragan, we're
in a bit of a rush. Big cottage plans.

Greg: We always seemed to do okay, but Towell just seemed to always be doing better. The autograph signings and Dominion Parking lot publicity events were always well attended... and kissing babies and signing the female fans sexposed buttocks and boobs were always worth so much more than the financial freedom we were entitled to as professional sportsters.

Dragan: No we never saw any [reports], but [Towell] always paid us, and on time. I didn't really care. He said we were doing well, I was appearing in main events, and Towell was always good for his word. My contract was never compromised.

Katherine: Looking back on the whole thing now it's totally absurd. It's like a great dream that you thought was real, but then you realize it was a dream but then you really realize it was reality. Then it freaks you out. Jesus! Black Ninja Seven! I remember the first time I saw him I thought to myself holy shit, look at that man. He moves like a cat. I bought all his merchandise for my friends. I've always had a thing for cats. At first I was skeptical, I mean, it's bowling for Christ sakes. I got into it though, fuck, more than I thought I could.

Alien #2:
(not interested at
all in Dragan)
Say Hi to Rob and Nik for us. Let's go get this shit off.

INT. Girls from behind, walking towards change rooms, peeling bits of fake skin off.

INT. Jerry patting Dragan on the back.

Jerry:
So that was fun, should be quite a good little spot.

Dragan:
Cool. Thanks.

Jerry:
You okay?

Dragan:
Just a bit sore from soccer.

"THESE DAYS I'M USING WCB LIKE MY ATM."
— GREG LEBELLE

Mumbling through breakfast Robert Towell broke his watch over his plate and pretended to crack it like an egg. The tiny gears and twitching second hand fumbled onto the plate of discarded toast and egg. He watched a custodian smear coffee across tiles.

"I can't get enough of that mop," he told Lebelle. Nikola returned from the bathroom only to inform her husband she was in fact late for a business meeting.

"Right, well, you have to do what keeps you informed. I'll see you Wednesday, Greg and I have business of our own. We have to get to *Total Sports* before they go to press for their next issue. This is crucial."

"I know, but they have the ad and are going to run it, you know the advertising editor right?"

"It's not just that, we're going to find some other outlets, bigger sponsors. This thing is growing. That's why I just destroyed my watch, I'm not living under the structure of physical reality any longer because it's wrong, there can be no rules for such a mind, such desire, such new inventive throngs of absolute fanaticism. As for *Total Sports*, I haven't received any confirmation. It's only a seven-hour drive. I need to just kick this thing as far as it will go."

"Do what you have to do, I'll save you some Easter dinner."

"Right, the ham and squash, the potatoes and jelly beans. How I will miss it."

"Talk to you later. Nice to see you again, Greg," Nikola said and got up to leave. Robert kissed her quickly and squeezed her right bicep.

"You've been to the gym, I can tell. I better lift some cans of corn on the road to keep up."

"You better." Nikola twinkled her eye.

Greg Lebelle nodded goodbye and inhaled the last of his Marlboro cigarettes. Robert watched his wife leave the restaurant and turned his attention back to Greg.

"So you'll be back in a week?"

"Less, like three days. See you then."

"Cool by me, you know where to find me."

Host: So, answer the age old question, what came first, the bowler or the bowling alley?

Robert Towell: Neither. It was the promoter who came first.

Host: Not some progressive cave man throwing a rock at a pile of things?

Robert: I had toyed with the idea of crossovers, a sprawling saga of origins, having a huge art show with a domestic and sports context, a bathtub teeming with bowling balls. But that made me want to puke. And no one wants to pay to see that.

Host: So is your league five or ten...

Robert: Listen, there is no real purpose in classification, we play in America too, we use a lot of weapons, and fists, different ball sizes doesn't really come up at any meetings. Mainly we just try to elevate the head, stop nosebleeds, drop-toe-hold seminar here, aerial assault 101 survey course there, plus, how to cut a promo without cutting yourself. It's a spiritual quest.

Host: Have you ever thought about having women in WCB, in a fighting capacity?

Robert: I do think about women in bowling but we're a small operation. If we got more money I'd branch out. You see, I do have some experience in being totally right about everything. And I just think that it would be a media nightmare, the exploitation. I have not received any offers.

Host: What if someone challenged, let's say, your wife.

Robert: Well, again this sounds like a pitch for some sort of angle, and I'm not open to discussions about my wife entering the fighting world. It would be her decision, but again I think we're just speculating on all these things, and it's just for the narrow amusement of this interview, which is gross, of course for everyone involved, mostly me.

Host: Are you a bowling *artiste* then?

Robert: I've been called a lot of things in my life, and earlier this morning, but no, I don't do portraits of bowling alleys. I have a parasitic relationship to bowling. I understood why I was there, as a young kid, I mean, I understood what I was doing, why I was there each week, but in the bigger picture, I didn't understand why "it" was there.

Host: By "it" you mean bowling?

Robert: Yes. You're on fire now!

Host: Robert, why is World Championship Bowling so violent?

Robert: Why not? Bowling needs to be put out of its commercial misery. This is going to blow-up and make a lot of people a lot of money. To be fair, I provide quality control for the world of professional bowling. It's quite gross actually, to watch bowling on television. It's worse than the dental network, or reverse crafts network where you watch someone unmake a quilt for seventy three hours, talking about their cats.

WCB publicity still.

GREG LEBELLE'S APARTMENT

TORONTO, ONTARIO
NOVEMBER 26, 1998

Greg Lebelle had called Robert Towell early in the morning and asked him over for coffee and bagels. Robert arrived around 10:30 AM and was buzzed up to Lebelle's apartment.

"How are things? You already down with this week's schedule?"

"Well, no, I mean, things are not so good right now," Lebelle said.

"Work related?"

"Yeah."

"Okay, so what do you want to do, you need some time off?"

> "LEBELLE WAS MOTIVATED, I COULD TELL THIS WAS HIS CALLING, HIS FATE. I NEVER THOUGHT THOUGH, SHIT I HAVE TO REPLACE LEBELLE, IT WAS MORE LIKE I HAD TO CHANGE MY LIFE AS WELL, START IN A NEW DIRECTION. THAT'S WHAT NO ONE UNDERSTOOD, HOW WE ALL INFLU-ENCED EACH OTHER'S LIVES."
> — ROBERT TOWELL

"Well, look it's all fucked, the Ministry of Health has this 'restructuring plan' for detox services and it's really going to mess things up."

"So they're closing detox centres?"

"Yeah, it's a funding thing, but that's what everyone says when things get closed."

"Sorry to hear that," Robert said, taking a quick sip of the coffee Lebelle had poured for him.

"So there's a ton of meetings I have to go to, and I'm going to be missing some house shows and that taping on Friday, I can't do it."

"That's fine. We'll work around it. How many centres are getting closed?"

"Don't know, they haven't said for sure but they've named two that are shutting down in like, three weeks, even though the centres are already overwhelmed and in high demand."

"That really sucks," Robert said, noticing for the first time how Lebelle's focus had shifted completely. There was no fraternal sentimentality, no boastful sports ego. This shift was permanent it seemed, unalterable.

"Well, I hope things work out for the sake of these programs."

"Yeah, thanks. Not much we can do, but we're going to be in talks with the city hopefully by Monday afternoon. We need to strategize a response to the cuts. Look, I'll talk to you soon, thanks for stopping by."

"Sure, no problem Greg, thanks for your time."

WCB BOWLBRAWL III

Cornwall Bowling Palace
Cornwall, Ontario
April 9, 1999

Turn: Motion of the hand and wrist toward pocket area at point of ball release.

Umbrella ball: A high hit on the nose resulting in a strike.

Under: Professional bowling score below 200.

Up the hill: Refers to coaxing a ball over a high board into the pocket.

Venting: Drilling a small hole (not a finger hole) to relieve suction on the thumb hole.

Washout: The 1-2-10 or 1-2-4-10 for right-handers and the 1-3-7 or 1-3-6-7 for lefties.

Water in the ball: A weak ball, one that leaves an 8-10, 5-7 or 5-10.

"I've been worrying about this, our whole sequel debacle, the media only wants to run what is new, not what is better. Even if we're providing a superior product, are we new? Forget relevant," Robert Towell spoke with a verve Jerry Tomlin had not seen in a few months. This feisty chainsaw was the Robert Towell that Tomlin had known since childhood, the same Towell he knew the day they both auditioned for the part of Michael Pumpkin. Robert Towell pulled his musty aviator glasses up from around his neck and began to shout with Herculean fortitude: "This sort of match has a real summer feeling to it." He clutched a blue ink drawing he had made earlier in the week. The sketch outlined the format of the controversial ladder match. Jerry Tomlin pretended not to hear him and continued to arbitrate the tension between the cast, crew and Towell, whose poisonous outlook and neurotic overtures of late were affecting the morale of the WCB product. "Everyone is clear with the rules right, they know the spots?"

"Yes," Tomlin said, trying not to snap. "I've talked to nearly everyone backstage. You and I doing play-by-play?"

"Yeah, maybe Clay will help us out too. I think Godfrey and Binner might actually show up in the free-for-all. It's gonna be chaos." Towell paused, then tossed the drawing into the air, and began barking commands, instructing his stage hands to remove all the balls from the surrounding lanes and secure the bowling bag on a hook sixteen feet above lane sixteen.

Jerry Tomlin reviewed the rules with Towell: "There's a ladder. Whoever can climb to the top, unhook the bowling bag from the hook suspended above the lane, get the ball, and then knock down a pin will capture the WCB championship. Right?"

"Yes, good. I feel good. No. I feel great."

"Good. Don't worry. I know you're worried because of the Greg factor, but this match is so unique, we don't need him."

"Yeah, I feel good about the spot."

"We've got about seven people ready for their run-in cues, two Ninjas, a bunch of extras…"

"And how's the champ?"

"He's ready, he's practicing his angry rebuttal about his soccer team being banned from lane-side."

"Good," Robert Towell said, removing a small vial filled with an off-white substance from his jacket pocket.

WINTERS PULLS OUT!
VIKING CONDOMS WON'T RESIGN WITH WCB

FROM 1BOWLING.COM

More bad news for WCB. Citing irreconcilable differences, Michelle Winters, head of Viking condoms, says her company won't be sponsoring any WCB programming in the future. Ms. Winters said in a recent interview: "In this age of terrorism, I found it really inappropriate that WCB's marketing team wanted to use a sword through a bowling ball as 'our' logo. Not only was the violence already implicit in the name, but the gothic cult fascination with the condoms has developed to such an extent that many people are willing to follow anything Viking makes, so long as it hints you can get laid. Also, the violence in the WCB was getting out of control. I don't approve of the creative direction the WCB is taking at this time. The violence isolates an entire consumer bracket, namely the victims of terrorist fear-mongering who can't take any more assault weapons on TV." Jerry Tomlin, representing WCB, said he was "surprised" that Viking condoms felt they had to pull out so early. Currently WCB has pulled back several of its promotional vignettes and products that cross-promote Viking.

For the first time in WCB history, Internet bowling reporters were allowed backstage and at production meetings. 1BOWLING.COM reporter Alexandra Houston-Smith was being encouraged to "leak angles and outcomes," according to Tomlin, because it was the first Lebelle-less BOWLBRAWL event, and WCB were not banking on high numbers for the buy-rate. Of course management didn't tell Momchilo when he complained of "Internet spies" asking him questions backstage. Tomlin simply assured the champion it was for a new journalism tolerance initiative, and left it at that.

The match splattered into reality, with a red spotlight glow swivelling on lane sixteen, the folded ladder nestling up front, the suspended bowling bag with the ball inside, awaiting its one-pin fate.

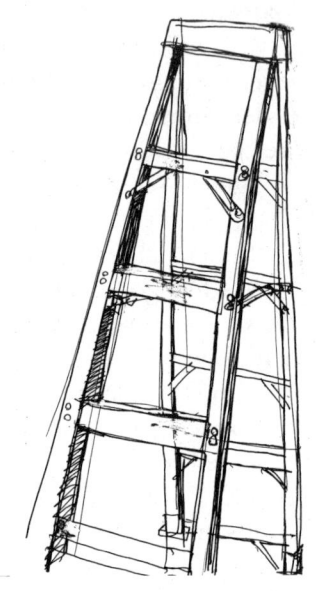

Towell sketch from Bowlbrawl III planning meeting, March 1999.

"Here is the reigning and defending WCB champion, 'Hollywood' Dragan Momchilo," the announcer boomed.

"Here comes our hero," Towell said with a smarmy cackle, as Momchilo sauntered into the alley, the Serbian flag draped around his neck.

"That's gonna piss off someone," Tomlin said casually. The play-by-play duo was joined by Clay Shallaghan, who tried to interject into the frenzy.

"So who came up with the idea for this match?"

"Well, that would be me Clay, but what a testament it is to this sport that we can settle things with such a complex notion, don't you agree?"

The loudspeaker boomed and a voice from the backstage area began: "And now, to announce his opponent, here is WCB owner, Robert Towell."

Jerry Tomlin had a surprised look on his face when the spotlight turned bright yellow and swarmed the WCB broadcast desk. In the spotlight Robert Towell stood up, removed his headset and clasped a microphone. He stared with disgust at the champion. He turned to the crowd and a big smile hatched across his face. "Tonight fans, we're giving you a big surprise. Because our hero, your hero, Dragan Momchilo, your champion, is going to defend his championship against... the world!"

With that, the WCB locker room emptied out. "And just so everyone knows what we discussed yesterday at the contract signing, NO SOCCER PLAYERS ARE ALLOWED IN THE BUILDING!"

As Momchilo's jaw dropped, indoor fireworks cackled across the bowling alley landscape. The two Ninjas made their way to centre stage. Following them was Jordan Binner looking ready for a fight. Following them were half a dozen extras hired out especially for the ladder match.

"This is going to be a tough night for Momchilo!"

Momchilo acted on instinct, grabbing the ladder and bunting the two Ninjas in the gut with the hard metal ends. He then lifted the ladder above his head and threw it down across both Ninja's backs.

"Momchilo is starting the offensive early, which is a great strategy."

"We'll see Tomlin, we'll see. There are just too many competitors, and his lungs are weak from smoking. He won't be able to climb that ladder without someone pushing him off," Towell added.

At the seven-minute mark Momchilo had knocked out six different bowlers, most of them the inexperienced extras. "These men are not up to the task," Tomlin cried.

"I haven't even heard of these bowlers before Towell, who are they?" Clay Shallaghan asked.

"Never mind. They come from good homes, and I assure you, they don't get accused of stealing sugar," Towell snapped.

"Hollywood" Dragan Momchilo slammed the ladder into Jordan Binner's chest and began to set up the apparatus for his climb to the bowling bag.

"Momchilo is setting up that ladder, he's trying to end this match!"

"We'll see about that," Towell said, giving a hand signal.

From the backstage area, pushing a wheelbarrow full of cinderblocks, Dale Godfrey stopped to wave to the crowd who were cheering him extensively. "It's Dale Godfrey and this place just went nuts," Tomlin cried. "We haven't seen him in action since the infamous chainsaw incident."

"Dale, come on, quit posing," Towell ordered.

Momchilo, unaware of the emergence of his estranged

Momchilo with Dale Godfrey backstage at BOWLBRAWL III.

friend Dale Godfrey, made his way up the rungs of the ladder accompanied by a series of cheers. He was inches away from touching the bowling bag when the ladder gave way.

"Oh my, this is disturbing, Momchilo has fallen!" Tomlin cried.

Godfrey dumped the cinderblocks from the shallow belly of the wheelbarrow and proceeded to manipulate the champion's vulnerable body. The crowd booed as Towell removed his headset and joined Godfrey in front of the lane.

"The dismantling of Dragan Momchilo seems to be unstoppable," Tomlin cried. "We saw moments ago, the champ pushed off the ladder, and backstage other bowlers, too injured to continue in tonight's main event, are being shipped out of here on stretchers. And now this, this appalling display of unsportsmanlike... oh my!"

Clay was getting the hang of the play-by-play: "Folks if you are just joining us now, you are in for some disturbing images. Cover the eyes of your children. It would appear as if WCB champion 'Hollywood' Dragan Momchilo has been put out of commission. If you watch this replay, from just moments ago, you can hear Towell instructing Godfrey to push Momchilo off the ladder. He landed on the ball return where Godfrey proceeded in smashing not one, but two cinderblocks over the young man's exposed knees. Look at that sick grin on Towell's face."

"It's like the anvil falling on the coyote or something," Tomlin interjected. Towell laughed and walked backstage in triumphant disgust, for once again, he had gutted Momchilo. "They're climbing either side of the ladder, it's Black Ninja Seven, it's Dragan Momchilo. Who will get to the

bowling ball first?" Tomlin shouted.

From the bottom rung, watching his counterpart struggle with the champ, Black Ninja Six made his mark felt. Six lunged at Momchilo's leg, clamping it to the side of the ladder.

"What's next, what more can happen tonight?"

Just then, like the pulling of an unwilling tooth, the moment became too much, until it gave way. "The Ninjas are injecting Momchilo with something."

Tomlin later recalled: "I remembered Towell talking to the Ninjas earlier in the night about a big swerve but I was completely in the dark about the novocaine. It took me by surprise, which I'm sure was Towell's intention. Steroids is one thing, but..."

Meanwhile Binner and Godfrey were plotting to take the Ninjas out of the equation. They stacked two folding tables onto one another in front of the ladder and waited patiently.

Black Ninja Six, who had administered the drug, told Seven to release Momchilo's leg from his grip. "He's gonna feel it soon, watch," Six said.

The guileless Ninja attack worked, Momchilo couldn't stand on the rung because his left leg was numb, and he began to waver. Black Ninja Six began to pummel the right leg.

"He's working on that strong leg," Tomlin cried.

The perfidious cloud of opponents continued to destroy the champion, but his hands still worked. As he tumbled awkwardly from the ladder, he took the metal into his hands and began to shake the ladder until it fell with him on the edge of the foul line, toppling Seven.

Backstage Towell watched the action on a monitor. *I can't stand this anymore.* Turning to an assistant he summoned his car. Soon he'd be back in Nikola's armpit.

Back at the play-by-play desk Jerry Tomlin wiped away the blood from his monitor with his tie. "If you think the competition at last year's BOWLBRAWL was cut-throat, just wait until you see this replay, again this is not for the weak at heart. BOWLBRAWL III promised pain, and with more injuries sustained in the first ten minutes than all the injuries at the last two tournaments combined, the emergency room will be stock full of WCB employees tonight, I assure you."

Something in Momchilo snapped. He chewed through the wiring in his foggy brain, kicked his feet, stomped on the ground, and tried to get the sensation back in his leg. "Momchilo is rising, he's still clenching that fallen ladder, preventing anyone from getting that ball," Clay said earnestly.

Black Ninja Six jumped up on the ball return. Momchilo was now on his knees, but managed to administer a low-blow between Black Ninja Seven's open legs which fluttered in a frenzy of blurred black cotton. Binner caught a Momchilo knuckle in the throat, and then, the finisher. "Momchilo is going for his signature move, 'The Dragan's Edge'. He's got Binner up and... oh my!" Tomlin cried.

With Binner out, Momchilo took the ladder and began to line up the Ninjas. "He keeps knocking them down, and pushing them into the gutter of the lane, like he's butting out cigarettes," Tomlin said.

With his opponents cut and frightened, "Hollywood" Dragan Momchilo set up the ladder and began to climb. Jordan Binner scaled the ladder from the other side. "Momchilo is racing now... wait he's reaching into his shorts, he's got something."

"Dragan you're not going to get that ball, this match is mine," Binner said with a hiss.

"I don't think so Jordan," Momchilo replied, and threw a handful of sugar into the young man's eyes, causing him to grip the ladder for balance.

"These guys hate each other," said Clay, mastering the obvious.

"Momchilo has reached the bowling bag... he's unzipped it... he's got the ball... he's going down that ladder..."

Before throwing the ball and securing victory, Momchilo looked at Binner, still on the ladder wiping sugar from his eyes. With a demonic grin, Momchilo put the ball down in front of him and pushed the ladder over, causing Binner to crash through two tables.

"Pieces of that table are everywhere, this is heinous, this is insanity, this is BOWLBRAWL! Now Momchilo is rolling... Oh no, a gutter."
No one had any idea how to react to this unscripted moment.

"What happens now Jerry?" Clay asked.

"This is awkward. I guess he'll have to wait for the ball return. It's not like Jordan is getting up."

"Is he even moving?"

"He's breathing. Ah, there we go. Momchilo has knocked down a pin on his second throw... he's won! Momchilo has retained the WCB championship, in what can only be described as the most brutal match in WCB history!"

"That was awesome, really brutal, although I can not condone what has just transpired. I wonder what the board will say about this," Clay Shallaghan said.

Jerry Tomlin, caught up in the energy of the gasping crowd: "Jordan Binner laid out unconscious by those tables. The Ninja's carted off one by one. And our champion, Dragan Momchilo, victorious, unstoppable, quite possibly the most dangerous man in our sport today, has come out on top. We'll see you all at DEVASTATION."

Greg Lebelle was back at WCB headquarters in Toronto, Ontario Tuesday. He sat quietly in front of a small television monitor, taking notes on a yellow legal pad while sifting through tons of old WCB footage for the soon-to-be released DVD chronicling his career.

"So far it's going really well," Lebelle said. "There's a good team of people here to get all the right clips together. The next two days will be real tight."

Lebelle also appreciates the buzz his name still generates. His meeting with Robert Towell earlier this month triggered an incredible reaction from Internet and bowling fans. "I appreciate that nobody has forgotten me," Lebelle said. "It's the whole reason for the DVD."

Lebelle also made it clear that the DVD will not only serve as a testament to his legendary career, but indirectly pay homage to many of the WCB superstars he was able to work with during his time at the company. "I hope this DVD will do justice to the great guys I had matches with," Lebelle said. "This is my way of showing that they're still a part of my story."

Lebelle with Jordan Binner. Screen capture from WCB DVD.

WCB HEADQUARTERS

Toronto, Ontario
August 8, 1999

"Oh fuck, you've got to be kidding me, just plead guilty for Christ sake, it was what, a two, three-punch fight?" Towell said into the phone, slamming the receiver down onto the cradle. "Fucking psychopath!"

"Who was that?" Nikola asked, trying to calm his anger.

"Oh that? Just my employee of the month."

The couple and all the WCB board members had assembled for what would be the last formal meeting of Towell's company, World Championship Bowling. By this time he was slowly dismantling a lot of the day-to-day tasks of WCB, and focussing on exploiting the brand in a way that was not time sensitive.

"Greg's thinking of retiring. These are human beings. We have to be honest with ourselves, they aren't actors, and this is no longer a sport. It pains me to do this, but I think it's over. I mean, technically, Lebelle's next match is against the Province of Ontario."

"What?" Nikola gasped.

"He got wasted one night, this new job, it's getting to him. He knocked some guy out. Says he thought the guy was Dragan. I'm not joking, I'm not making this up. I mean, that's his defense. It's a real mess. Most of you don't know that he's also a harm reduction worker. He gives out clean needles to street kids, screens for crack pipes, you know, kid's stuff. Lately he's been talking like he wants to live on the streets. I don't think we can make this an angle anymore, I don't think we can reflect this. His life isn't sports entertainment anymore. It's just sad, honourable but sad."

"So what are we going to do?"

"Fold."

"What?"

"We aren't making Harm Reduction Lebelle, comes with clean syringe."

"So what do you suggest?"

"I've already suggested it, and told our shareholders, our sponsors, web providers, hosts, and manufacturers. We are cutting down on production. No more costs. Find yourselves new jobs, hobbies, take up golf. Leave me the fuck alone. After DEVASTATION next month, World Championship Bowling is shelved. I'm going to see a publisher about my memoirs and we'll move some T-shirts but no more."

"Shelved my ass. Don't you read the papers?" Tomlin asked, his face flush with concern. "These bowler hunters or whatever the fuck they are, started their own campaign, they want to hunt you down."

"I know, I got the deets from Fan 590 this morning. Big deal."

"I think it's trouble," Tomlin said.

"Well of course it's trouble. It's also PR, costs us nothing. Nevertheless, I've decided to release a statement on WCB.COM in regards to the hunters. It will simply state: *To all those concerned with WCB's whereabouts, as well as my own, to those concerned that these rural hunters who by no coincidence are ex-bowlers of the obese persuasion, have claimed to have, in their gluttonous state, reduced me and my company to the shame of dwelling night and day in the underground caverns of Peterborough, Ontario, I assure you, this is not the case, and that I'm currently very well dressed and do not, nor does any WCB employee, live underground. Best regards, Robert Towell, Owner, WCB.*"

"That's catchy. But they hate you."

"But it will get some local media coverage. We can push the product. That counts, right?"

FAXES FROM FINAL MEETING OF WCB

10:17 AM: *Rob, yes I would like to stay in tuch with u... their are manny I wish not to be in tuch with ...my life is verry good now Judy and I are doing verry well for our selfs we have a big house a truck and planing to buy new truck in spring or summer ..my oldest son came to live with us he been here over a year now ...my masonry bizznes has taken off doing well finley but actuley to bizzy...mony good ...but time to my self would allso be good...we live in the beache's 401 kinston rd..toronto ...ok hope your doing well ..Dale.*

1:24 PM: *Dear Mr. Towell. We have reviewed your request and make the following recommendations: 1. By looking at a game box, a consumer has to be able to tell what the game is about instantly, without reading the back or even looking at the title. This box art does not do that. 2. Good luck, no one will touch this. Why would anyone advance money/give you a cut on the back end when they could just develop their own game using the general concept without paying you a dime? Every development team in the world has their own pet ideas, why would they want to work on someone else's vision/masterpiece? 3. The only way you will get this game made is if you put a team together and head up the project, producing a compelling prototype of some kind. No one is going to give someone without industry experience a penny without AT LEAST a prototype. Frankly, even with a prototype, it will be a very tough sell — the industry experience is key.*

WCB DEVASTATION

O'CONNOR BOWL
EAST YORK, ONTARIO
SEPTEMBER 17, 1999

> **ARMBAR:** In bowling, the arms are more important than anything else. Even on the ground, lying down, attempts can be made to knock down pins, which is usually the goal. The armbar compromises this drive.

Robert Towell looked at the cage being assembled by the crew, and chewed on a stack of nearby plastic straws. He reacted immediately to the unfortunate environment he had recast himself in. He had always reassessed his situation since starting World Championship Bowling, but this was deeper, because he was now a cog, a part of the system, the system he had forced down the throat of the sport itself. Once again, he was specimen. "It freaked me out completely, as if I could smell the gingerale coursing through the dead arteries and veins and nasal passages of my late coach," he would later comment.

His present setting tongued at his growing wound: the scent, the chewed shoelaces, the stale oxygen, impure stains of multi-coughed dust balls, the briny dirt lodged under finger and toenails, hidden somewhere in the palm of the dead. The dead, Towell thought, must be buried somewhere nearby, listening. The malt vinegar was in boxes, waiting to drench the food of the culinary weak. The bowling troughs prepared themselves for the evening's locusts. He studied the diced green flesh of the relish packages, remembering without fondness the countless foul hot dogs that morphed and churned inside his boy stomach.

To make matters worse, "Hollywood" Dragan Momchilo, fresh from a soccer practice and umpteen other unspoken suburban errands, paced nervously in front of his boss as the sun flossed the dirt in the parking lot for the final minute of the day. There was talk of sharing a plate of steaming fries in ketchup, a plan that did not materialize. Robert Towell could not look up from the relish autopsy.

"Um, how's it going?" Momchilo said, putting his gym bag down on the table. "What's happening?" Momchilo coughed, and repeated himself. "What's happening?" The men were underground, together, gelled in a suspension of fear and anxiety, and Momchilo was the first to share. "Rob I feel crazy, these dreams are getting to me."

The alchemy of Robert's own insane words followed Momchilo's confession. Robert could feel himself breathing slower, taking in the elements of the underground world around him, but not understanding. His own focus was fogged by the swelling tears he had to restrain. But he put on a brave face, *just another hour or so of this illusion,* he thought. *This will be over.*

"Don't worry about tonight, you'll be fine," Robert said, trying to undo the knots in his stomach with his mind. "You need to lighten up."

"I just feel…"

"Eat something, you think and think and it goes nowhere and I suffer, the world suffers, you spiral into the infinity of your own limited joy ride. I mean, all your focus is in one stupid area where you put all your thoughts, you pile them all right there at the back of your leg and say 'Look at the back of my leg, it's full of my thoughts, it's like a pregnant vacuum cleaner and it's getting really hard to walk.'"

Momchilo tried to feel better, but was clearly talking to the wrong man. He tried to move the discussion forward. "I mean, I thought if I did those condom commercials, with the alien girls in their panties and they look like aliens. I thought it would make me confront it, and I could laugh, but it's just getting worse."

"What? The dreams?"

"Yes."

"Are you still reading those trashy horror novels?"

"Only on the bus."

"Stop reading that stuff. Those aren't self-help books."

"So what is the finish tonight?"

"The same. You lose."

"What?"

"Look, there is some bad shit going down in a few months, really bad. I was out with Greg a few weeks ago, no one knows this but you and I. He's going to jail."

"When did you decide I had to lose?"

"Last week. But I figured if I told you then, you'd just walk. Please do this for me, I made a huge mistake. I'm sorry. I saw your soccer contract, you're renewing with them. I figured, this could be it, for awhile."

"You're giving the title to someone who is going to show up in court holding a trophy like a psychotic clown."

"I know. But look, if I *don't* give him the title, and this *still* happened, he'd probably come after you. I can't tell how much Greg thinks is real and how much he thinks is fake. If he shows up tonight, and let's say he lost, imagine, just before the trial, he'd be obsessing about this, he'd be like, *If I'm going down, I'm taking you all with me.* At least this way, he goes into his bowling trial as the champion. Better than you having it, and him breaking into your house while you slept. Then he'd really kill your grandmother."

With this sort of rationale, Robert knew things had gone too far. He looked forward to the finality, the last frame, the final nail in the coffin.

"But I've been loyal, I've done signings, posed for doll manufacturers."

"You did that on your own volition, they didn't need you to pose for them, in fact, they wondered what you were doing at the plant."

"You are punishing me for being an athlete."

"No, if Black Ninja Six was champion I'd make him drop the title too."

"You can't compare me to the Ninjas."

"You could be my champion after this night is over, but those soccer guys throw you a couple of extra thousand bucks and you show up on the field with my WCB championship and then throw the title on the ground and kick it. It would be great for them, their ratings would go up."

"I would never do that to you. And besides, soccer doesn't rely on that sort of drama."

"See, they've already brainwashed you. And you'd do it, if they paid you enough. You said yourself you need the money."

"But they don't care that I bowl."

"Look, we'll figure something out, at least this way, with me screwing you yet again out of the title, you will have the fan's support. We have to take the heat off of Lebelle as the trial goes down. This will be a night he can at least say the game treated him fairly. Because Lord knows Dragan, he's about to get fucked by Satan himself. He chose this path, we can at least butter his slide down to Hell. Anything else you want to complain about?"

"Yeah, at that house show in Banff, you had my ex-girlfriend in on a match where I was the referee, and then she was the special guest run-in attacker. You caught my reaction on film and the whole fucking crew was in on it."

"But it wasn't on a pay-per-view, just a bunch of hicks in Alberta saw it. And besides, I did that because you're a terrible actor. It was the only way to make you look like the babyface you are. You were pissed but more paranoid than angry. It suited your character."

"Fuck this."

"Exactly. You are unstable, just like Lebelle. Take some time off if you want. We'll work on a script."

"Yeah, whatever Towell, all I know is I move more merchandise, more toys, more T-shirts and more hot-line charges than anyone else here at

WCB. So I don't know why you keep lying to me."

"Dragan, do you understand this is a business to me, not a sport? Do you really think people would watch this show if it was based on skill? That is what the PBA is for. You want to try out for that league go ahead, quit smoking. In my company you can smoke, you can swear, kick and fight your way into the hearts of millions. Greg won't ever defend that title again. He's going to jail and that is PR money can't buy."

"So you are giving him the title based solely on the fact that it will get publicity?"

"No. Also because I don't trust you. You're changing, you're becoming a very talented athlete in a real sport. And I can't replace you, but I also can't build my company around you any longer. It'll work out. Trust me."

EXT. Bowling alley. Placard reads:

WCB PRESENTS
DEVASTATION
LIVE TONIGHT ON PAY-PER-VIEW

INT. WCB desk in front of lane sixteen.

Jerry:
This is not going to be pretty. It has come to this, these three men, possibly the most lethal individuals to ever step inside of a bowling alley have decided to settle their differences once and for all.

Dale:
This is going to be hell. I've never seen a cage inside of a bowling alley, and being this close to it, it's really something.

Jerry:
The most barbaric match in this sport has just been realized. Robert Towell has been heard backstage muttering: "Don't fear the cage, fear me." I've called a lot of WCB matches over the past couple of years, but nothing comes close to this. These three men are going to Hell, and we are all going to Hell. At DEVASTATION, prepare to be... devastated.

The rules are simple. Three men will enter a cage with three balls. They have to register a single point, and then exit the cage. The first man out of the cage, after registering at least one point, is the winner.

INT. Backstage in a small office. Robert Towell closes the door and begins his private meeting with "Hollywood" Dragan Momchilo.

Dragan:

Fuck. I don't need this.

Robert:

I'm sorry you are taking this so personally. You're acting like an ungrateful kid.

INT. Dragan leaving the room.
INT. Close up on Robert Towell's glare.
INT. Hallway. Dragan fading down the hallway.
INT. Robert Towell changes for the match.

Robert:

(monologue)
It would be my first bowling match in over a decade; the last thing I wanted was to have contact with a bowling ball, the thought alone made my fingers burn, or at least trickle imaginary hot water. I felt my neck crawl with maggots, I could smell the death-scented footwear, trying to charm me into surrender. I'll never put on a pair of bowling shoes again. I'd rather starve.

INT. Flashback of young Robert Towell picking up a bowling ball. The adult Towell watches the younger version of himself in horror.

Robert:

The fact that I was scheduled to be in this match, to walk on the surface of the lane itself made my stomach boil. I could feel the flesh inside my stomach, as if it were being peeled slowly by a paring knife. I saw rust floating in ice water and I was thirsty.

INT. Robert in the changing room mirror, sweating, doing up his shirt, slowly exhaling, water dripping down his face.

Robert:
> But, if this was to be the final WCB match ever I felt, at the very least, the owner should be represented. I didn't want the last memory of me in the bowling world to be a sulking teenage wimp, walking out of the building like a sour bitch. That was years ago anyway. This would be a great finish, and I was honestly looking forward to facing my two top roster stars, and ripping into them, one last time. I could almost smell the blood, how it would clog the grains of the lane, and how Dragan's decaying lungs, assisted by his continual smoking, would be crushed like a barbecued chicken rib cage.

INT. Bowling alley. Crowd fills up, cheering fans buying merchandise, T-shirts, posters with Dragan, Greg & Robert's face behind bars.

It was Robert Towell's last minute scattering that lead to six hired hands to pass out cheap plastic combs to every ticket holder. The crowd filed in, nasty wads of spit hurtled towards the ground as if part of a natural seasonal shedding. Some patrons could not be controlled, no matter how many free combs were handed out at the door. "It was comb day, but it didn't work, no one cared, it was the nineties," Towell mocked in a micro-cassette interview marked *No Good Sunny Boy Vol. 6.*

ROBERT TOWELL RECALLS: "THERE WAS NO LOGIC IN THE MOMENT, JUST THE CHISELING OF FINGERNAILS RIPPING THROUGH T-SHIRT COLLARS, AND THE SLAMMING OF CLOSED FISTS INTO TEMPLES, THE THROAT THROTTLING BALLET OF CRUELTY, AND THE AFTERSHAVE REMOVING FACE-SLAPS."

Usually used for safety purposes on a construction site, the sectional cages were painted black and made of steel and mesh. Each section was eight feet high by ten feet wide, and bordered the sides and front of lane sixteen.

Inside, Towell, Momchilo and Lebelle stalked one another: three horror film divas ready for a blood buffet.

At the WCB broadcast desk, Jerry Tomlin prepared to call the main event as Dale Godfrey waved to the fans. "I'm Jerry Tomlin along with

Dale Godfrey, and as you can see in this long shot, all three WCB superstars are already inside the cage, and all three men are ready for this, the main event for the WCB title, here at DEVASTATION!"

Dale Godfrey: "I think we're just waiting for the official word from the time keeper... no we're underway."

The three men closed in on one another, the heat from the audience exceeded that of the crew, who were propping open the doors backstage.

"I never thought I'd see a cage match in a bowling alley," said Godfrey.

"Well, that's a given," Tomlin said. "Folks, we're underway. This is WCB DEVASTATION, and the first time a steel cage has been implemented in a sanctioned bowling match."

Dragan Momchilo was quick to retaliate from the initial melee, and picked up a nearby ball only to be blindsided by a light slap in the face, followed by a staggering attack on his stomach by a Lebelle fist. "This is the end," Tomlin announced, "this is going to end it all, Momchilo is on his knees, Lebelle is wrapping his fist in chain!" Tomlin declared.

As Lebelle pounded his chained fist into the champion's stomach, Momchilo dropped the ball and fell to his knees.

"He's dropped the ball," Godfrey cried. "Dragan is down, holding his stomach."

On his way down, clenching his stomach, Lebelle ran his hand through the fallen competitor's hair, revealing with disgust to the crowd the amount of gel Momchilo was using. Lebelle picked up a plastic comb, one of several tossed into the cage and ran the teeth over his bald skull.

"That's disgusting!" Jerry Tomlin cried, wiping his dark blond hair from his eyes.

Lebelle picked Momchilo up by the neck and clenched Towell in his other hand, throwing both men head-first into the steel cage.

"Momchilo is busted open."

"That's gotta hurt," Jerry Tomlin said.

Lebelle quickly pulled a pack of thumbtacks from his pocket and peppered the lane with the protrusions. "What the hell is he doing now?" Godfrey cried. "He's motioning to the cage, that unforgiving steel, and Lebelle is going for a pinfall here, he's going to secure his single point and qualify to escape this cage!"

Just before Lebelle released the ball from his grip Momchilo, with a thread of Ajax blood dribbling down his forehead, got to his feet and stood in front of his foe. "What's wrong, too tired?" Momchilo offered, followed by a wad of spit.

"Fuck you, and your grandma!" Lebelle snorted, and threw the ball at Momchilo's feet.

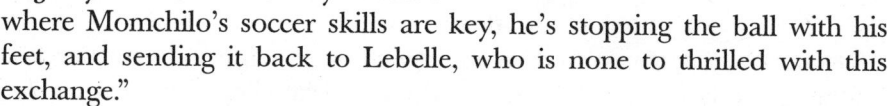

Jerry Tomlin: "Oh my! Here's where Momchilo's soccer skills are key, he's stopping the ball with his feet, and sending it back to Lebelle, who is none to thrilled with this exchange."

Robert Towell recalls the early stages of the cage match: "Our bodies seemed to migrate to one another, each shove, each taunt, claw, was another step in the fate pantomime. I knew that if I tried to replace them, it would not be the same. That was something I was thinking about, even with a pipe in my hand."

Meanwhile, Lebelle had set "Hollywood" Dragan Momchilo up for the missile-toes, baiting the champ to charge him by acting slightly winded.

"Oh my!" cried Tomlin. "Momchilo has fallen for the trap, his head landed hard on that modified leg sweep Lebelle calls missile-toes."

Knowing he would not remain undetected in the dance for long and sensing danger for his personal well-being, Robert Towell reached for a fire extinguisher which, in addition to sledge hammers, pieces of pipe, steel chairs, bats and other miscellaneous weapons, had been placed around the cage by stage hands before the match.

Quick to turn around, Towell clocked Lebelle in the centre of the forehead, sending him to the ground. "That was sick, that was unbelievable."

Lebelle stood up, took Towell by the throat and then the back of the head. "He's running the boss's head across that relentless steel, this is not going to be pretty."

Nikola Towell watched in horror on a small monitor in the back. *Please, just get out of there, let's go, get out of this. Please,* she thought to herself. She was not alone in anxiety, as most of the staff and crew, concerned about the outcome, had surrounded every available monitor in the back.

Inside the grip of Lebelle, Towell was not fairing very well. After the tenth time having his head buff the steel cage, Robert Towell managed to turn on the fire extinguisher, which sprayed his attacker, sending Lebelle to the floor.

"Momchilo is going for a pinfall here, but it looks as though Towell is on pace to deny him that chance!" Jerry Tomlin jeered.

"Oh, right in the face," Dale Godfrey cried, as Towell slammed the hard red steel into the champ's jaw. "That's going to slow him down."

Robert stood above both men, clenching the fire extinguisher and scanning the lane for opportunity, when Lebelle clipped his left leg out from under him. "Oh my, Towell is down!"

Jerry Tomlin continued: "After all the terrific pay-per-views and house shows we've seen here at WCB over the past few years, many wondered if these men could out-do themselves, and I think we have the answer right here," Tomlin said with a mixture of regret and pride.

"Lebelle has picked up the ball Momchilo dropped and launched it... the pin is down, he's clear to get out of the cage!" Tomlin cried.

"This could be over real soon, right Jerry?" Godfrey countered.

"That's right Dale."

Interrupting the pinfall attempts of his opponents, Lebelle provided swift kicks to their stomachs. The action moved into a desperate clawing melee. Momchilo kicked Towell in the stomach, grabbing the fire extinguisher from his hands, and struck his boss across the upper temple with the safety device. "I believe Towell may have caught some of those tacks on his way down."

"This is insane!" Godfrey shouted. The crowd behind him was foaming now, straining to see through the mesh.

"This match has reached a felonious level, these men seem hell bent on destroying one another," Tomlin added.

Lebelle was on his feet now, trying to make a bid for freedom.

"The boss is down!" Godfrey cried. "And Greg Lebelle is scaling the cage, right in front of our broadcast desk."

"Hollywood" Dragan Momchilo raced towards Lebelle's legs, hitting him with the extinguisher. Lebelle retaliated with a series of thick kicks, spitting down on the champion.

"I think the champ is going for plan B, he's going for a ball."

With a ball over his head, Momchilo looked at the pins, then turned with speed, ran towards Lebelle and launched the ball right into the small of the giant's back.

"Holy shit! I can't believe he just did that!" Dale Godfrey said, standing on his chair.

"Sit down!" Tomlin said, pulling the microphone from his face.

"Lebelle has fallen from the top of the cage!"

Momchilo dropped an awkward elbow on Lebelle and picked up the ball. As he released it, Robert Towell knocked the champ from the side with double-clasped knuckle and the ball landed in the gutter.

"Jerry, there's only one ball left, and Momchilo and Towell both have to get a pin down if they want to escape the cage!"

"Thanks Sergeant Obvious," Robert Towell shouted towards the WCB desk from inside the cage, before throwing his left knuckle into Momchilo's jaw.

Not a single body was still in his or her seat. Even the crew backstage fidgeted and shuffled back and forth, clenching one another's clothing in anxiety.

"Lebelle is up, and is heading straight for both men. He's taken them both out!" Godfrey cried. Lebelle then pulled a steel chair from the array of weapons and supplanted the champ's ankle into the folds of the legs.

"He's going to break the ankle," Tomlin warned. "Those steel legs are going to pinch down across the... oh my!"

Robert Towell sprung a high knee into the back of Lebelle, sending him into one of the walls of the cage. Lebelle's reaction was proactive, he kicked Towell in the guts and began to climb the cage.

"He's reaching for the top of the cage, he's going up and over, Lebelle keeps looking back as he climbs, trying to pull his wounded body over and out of this hellish battle."

On the ground Robert Towell and "Hollywood" Dragan Momchilo regained their composure, with

Momchilo being the first to his feet. He reached through the bars for the closest weapon, which turned out to be a heavy sledgehammer.

"I don't know if Momchilo has the strength to stop Lebelle, this looks like it's going to get really messy."

Now on his feet, Momchilo pointed at the pins, and with his other hand picked up the ball and knocked down three pins. "Momchilo has secured his quota, he's ready to leave the cage, but can he catch Lebelle?" Frothing in excitement Dale Godfrey tugged on his toque and bit his lip.

"He's got Lebelle's foot."

"At least he's not smoking."

"Meanwhile, let's not forget this company's owner, Robert Towell, who is now on his feet. He must keep these men from escaping if he wants to win. Folks remember, Robert Towell hasn't picked up a bowling ball in over ten years."

On the edge of the cage "Hollywood" Dragan Momchilo and Greg "Agamemnon" Lebelle ripped at any facial extremity they could find.

"Get back inside you stupid fuck," Momchilo screamed, hitting the bottom of the monster's chin with the sledgehammer, his mouth filled with Lebelle's hot fingers. "Fuck you and your grandmother too," Lebelle said, his throat fettered in Serbian fingerprints. "Give me this," Lebelle whispered, prying Momchilo's fingers from the throat of the hammer.

"They're fighting over that weapon, wait, it's dropped, it has hit the lane."

Momchilo gouged Lebelle's eye and pulled him back inside the cage by several rungs.

"Towell is up, he's charging the cage, wait, he's lifted up the sledge-hammer, oh my!"

The crowd swallowed its spit. The crew backstage turned their backs on the monitors momentarily. "Robert Towell has just connected the most edacious spinal wallop I have ever witnessed," Jerry Tomlin said with a shocked voice.

Robert Towell watched Momchilo drop like a dead house fly. He got down on his knees, a bit of blood spitting from his open forehead. He dripped over his fallen employee and whispered: "This is it, this is the big fucking pay-off. You'll thank me when this is over, it's the only real thing you've ever done, ever felt."

"That's fucked, I mean, that's all I can say."

"Incredible. I don't condone what Towell has done, but this is a night we surely won't forget."

"They won't be the same after this."

"How can you be, I mean, the human body is not designed for this type of punishment."

For the first time in his WCB career, Greg Lebelle had a look of horror on his face, unable to fully process what had happened. Perhaps in the midst of all the lights and attention, the knowledge that parts of the world were witnessing his every action, he could feel the glitter of anonymous eyes taking parts of himself away....

"But he's not done," Godfrey cried.

Robert Towell was now climbing the cage with the sledgehammer.

"I felt like I had it in my teeth, and I was climbing up the mast of a pirate ship to change a light bulb," recalls Towell.

"Right in the stomach, oh my God! That's it for Lebelle!" Tomlin said as Lebelle released his grip on the cage and fell, landing with a crash. "That did not look right, that fall may have finished Lebelle's career," Tomlin said in awe. Lebelle clenched his ankle, and spat an uneven wad of blood to the ground.

"Towell is pointing at Momchilo with that sledgehammer, he's climbing down from the cage."

Pirated dubs of the end of the match would be looped and downloaded online at fan sites throughout the evening: WCB owner Robert Towell clenching Dragan Momchilo by the back of the neck and hurtling him head-first into the pins, knocking them all down in the process. He finished off the young man with a drop-toe-hold, sending the champ head first into the fallen sledgehammer.

With Lebelle back on his feet, Momchilo disposed of, Robert Towell raced up the cage. "They're neck and neck, this is it, one of these men is going over," Tomlin said.

"This is too close."

A thumb to the eye, and a well-placed elbow to Towell's left cheek, allowed Lebelle to slip over the top of the cage and land on the alley floor.

Jerry Tomlin: "Greg Lebelle has touched the ground first, he's the champ, Lebelle has done it, and Dragan Momchilo has been left for dead, rammed headfirst into the pins by WCB owner Robert Towell."

"The winner of the cage match, and once again WCB champion, Greg 'Agamemnon' Lebelle!"

As Robert Towell kicked a handful of expired thumbtacks out of his path, he felt a shiver throughout his body. Greg Lebelle hoisted the trophy up over his head for the last time with dried blood fingerprints on his cheeks and neck. As the main lights went off, Towell sauntered over to

"Hollywood" Dragan Momchilo and helped him up off the ground. He was holding a fresh gash.

"How's it going?" Robert said.

"Just thinking," Dragan replied, his face red from the collision.

"Let's get out of here."

As the technicians took the cage apart, Lebelle and Momchilo chatted and shared strange memories. Towell said nothing as he witnessed his two gladiators formally surrender their friendship. *They were never meant to know one another, this underworld,* thought Towell, *this fakery, this sham of a sport, and within the prison of this fakery, their paths had been threaded, and were now unravelling.*

"I probably won't see you for awhile," Lebelle said, putting the trophy down on the ground, nodding to a photographer who was reloading.

"Yeah, I know. Good luck," Momchilo replied, holding a towel of ice to his forehead.

"How's soccer going?"

"Good. I'm semi-pro now. Lots of scouts in the stands these days. How's work?"

"Tough, I'm up at 6:00 AM, out on the street some nights until 5:00 in the morning, but I sleep here and there during the day. Some afternoons I have off."

"And it's for what again? Street Health?"

"Yeah, and a few other drop-in centres."

"Well, I'm sure I'll hear what happens," Momchilo said, trying not to say the word trial, but wanting to, trying not to think about the reality of the situation, the strange swerve in the storyline. "But call me soon."

"I will."

They would never have otherwise spoken, on a bus, streetcar, or in line at a vending machine – their separate lives were anything but comparable. And it was in this observation that Robert Towell detected the purity of their union; all of them, each and every cog was linked, a team of dysfunctional researchers, pining away at midnight for an answer, *why were we together?* Together they had found a new route in life, a new course, and had gone the distance. Without their bodies, WCB would have been a drunken bar napkin sketch. Technically, it was the last night Greg Lebelle would ever taste WCB gold, before the gold was tarnished and tagged for the courts.

It happened a month before DEVASTATION was booked. After going over some storylines Towell and Lebelle went out one night for a nightcap. "More like a ten gallon hat," recalls Towell. "So, after a few drinks, the groggy Lebelle, who was all sloppy and cement like, thick and heavy, was staggering into me, a wave of sweat, and he was just going on about his life and stress and I foolishly said, *Imagine if Dragan were here now,* and he just snapped, picked a fight with a stranger on King Street.

Ten minutes and six police officers later, Robert Towell witnessed his entire empire fettered in handcuffs and carted off in a white car, in his palm Lebelle's cellphone and house keys.

Outside the bowling alley, the crew and players nodded goodbye as the sun finally snapped off for the day.

That night Lebelle put his WCB championship trophy under his kitchen sink, next to the bleach, made himself a drink and with an arduous sigh, spent the early morning hours throwing darts into the photograph Katherine Cockshutt had taken in New Orleans. It was of a tomb. The surname on the stone read *Bowling.*

Photo courtesy of Katherine Cockshutt.

WCB HEADQUARTERS

Toronto, Ontario
September 21, 1999

"Okay guys, this is the last day you all work for me, so can we pretend like we're dedicated to detail? Lebelle is going to jail, we have no more suppliers, no sponsors, we're going out and we're going out large. We're going to drop WCB coupons from the skies, 50% off all merchandise. The coupons will be valid for the rest of the year. We have half a tank of gas left in the private jet, let's swing by the photocopy lounge, get some bright paper, and go nuts. And remember, since it's September, the world will only have until Christmas to cash in on these soon to be collector's items don't you think? As for the press release, you can't start with some flimsy invariable. I need drama from the beginning, something bigger than Bethlehem and those fucking reindeer. Right now, I mean, this flyer is as appealing as well, something entirely unappealing," Robert Towell commanded from atop his desk.

ROBERT TOWELL HAS GONE MAD!
WCB MERCHANDISE DISCOUNT SAVE 50%
Yes, I want to save on World Championship Bowling action figures, towels, bath soap and swimwear. I understand this coupon will expire by year's end.

"How can you describe one moment here in the first person voice and use my name above in the third-person? And what sort of garbage paper is it written on? And why am I dressed so poorly? Can't the sketch artist make me look like a millionaire for once in his fucking life? Should I just dictate this into a microphone and leave it to someone else? Forget the notes. Someone with a Polaroid, or how about that photo of me on the June issue of *WCB* where I'm holding the sixteen foot perch? That would be a good picture to use instead of this Monopoly line-art rip off. My idiot public deserves better."

GREG, YOU AND TOWELL GREW CLOSE IN 1998, AND DECIDED THE OUTCOME OF MOST OF THE MATCHES AT PAY-PER-VIEWS. MANY FEEL IT WAS THIS UNION THAT ENDED THE COMPANY. THEN THE TRIAL IN 2000, FURTHER TROUBLE FOR YOU, AND THE CALL FROM TOWELL, POST-TRIAL, WHO WAS STILL OBSESSED, STILL VENGEFUL AT THIS SPORT, HAD THE IDEA TO COME BACK AND INVADE THE PBA. WHAT WERE YOUR FEELINGS? DID YOU REALLY THINK YOU WOULD BE ABLE TO PULL IT OFF LIVE AT THE TRIAL, WITHOUT WCB BACKING YOU?

Greg: The strangest thing about life is that we may spend years and years playing for the public... kissing those babies... being icons and giants to the world of teenage fans, and sport connoisseurs... but one mistake, and all is forgotten. Like that joke about the ship builder who all his life made the best fishing boats in all of the village. He created from the best lumber the fastest, most sea-worthy vessels. For forty years he lived and worked in the community, building these boats for his sea-faring village but after getting caught fucking one sheep, drunk one night, and on just a passionate whim... he was no longer remembered as the world's greatest boat builder; instead... he is the guy who lives on the hill and is a sheep-fucker.

R obert Towell and Greg Lebelle walked along the University of Toronto campus, fresh from Lebelle's meeting with his legally appointed representative. Robert had waited outside in the hallway during the meeting, checking figures and scouring magazines for new investment tips.

They stopped for a can of pop at a hot dog stand.

"Can I ask you something? I mean, you haven't talked to me since you submitted your statement, and met with your lawyer. I don't really know what you're planning on telling the court, but I have been subpoenaed, I have to go."

"Why did you start this? Why did you pick us?" Greg Lebelle asked, thanking the hot dog merchant for the napkin with a nod.

Robert Towell was ready. "So what, we both get to ask questions and, there are... no answers, just two people, completely unable to figure out why they even know each other anymore?" Towell snapped, opening his can of Canada Dry. "If you have implicated WCB in your statement, I can't protect you. Your contract makes you liable during times when you are bowling, not when you're out getting pissed and picking fights."

WCB CHAMPION GREG LEBELLE vs THE CROWN

PROVINCIAL COURT
TORONTO, ONTARIO
APRIL 6, 2000

TELEPHONE POLES: Heavy pins.

THE FIRE'S OUT: Common expression used when a string of strikes comes to an end.

THIN HIT: A pocket hit when the ball barely touches the headpin.

300 GAME: A perfect 10-pin game consisting of 12 strikes in a row.

300 GAME JINX: It is customary when someone starts a 10-pin game with a string of strikes not to mention the possibility of scoring 300, which would "jinx" the player.

Nikola and Robert Towell were idling outside of Old City Hall; the Toronto seagulls did their best vulture impression. As Nikola slid out of the passenger seat, her white silk fifties bathing suit, which she wore as part of an ensemble, caught on a loose wire. Unhooking herself, she made her way around to the driver's seat as Robert took his briefcase into his sweating hand.

"Robert, are you all right?"

"Yes."

"You sure you don't want me to come in?"

"No. Just go to work, you'll be fine."

"I'm not worried about me, I've never seen you so stressed out."

"It's just that I have no idea what Lebelle's defense is in this, he's kept me in the dark for most of the meetings with the lawyer."

"It'll be over, remember, it's his trial, you're just doing what you're suppose to do."

"But I don't even know what that is. I can't go into the courtroom until everyone has testified, so it'll take all day I guess."

"Call me when it's over."

"I will Nikola."

Robert Towell prepped himself for what would be the most ridiculous moment in the history of anything, including bowling and manhood in general. As he would later recount in his memoir, in a chapter dedicated to the post-trial frenzy, Towell summed it up bravely: "It was like having my balls turned into a cartoon for seven hours and being forced to listen to them sing Christmas songs while everyone else was tanning on the lawn outside."

"The trial *Lebelle vs The Crown* will be heard today," Robert Towell said aloud. "Today is Thursday April 6, 2000. Live from Toronto, Canada. Okay, let's do this."

"Mr. Towell can you please describe to the court Mr. Lebelle's mood on the night in question?" ·
"He seemed fine."
"It didn't strike you as odd that he was drinking?"
"No. A lot of professional athletes drink." Robert was confused, and didn't know what was said during the past six hours and Greg was looking at him funny, sideways, why didn't he want any of the footage aired? This is so dumb.
"Was Mr. Lebelle angry? Or upset?"
"What's the difference between those two?"
"Mr. Towell, can you tell us about your bowling club?"
"We go bowling and film it, we do pay-per-views."
"Can you explain pay-per-view?"
"We rent out a bowling alley and broadcast it on the web or on local access cable. We charge a sur-fee for promotional airings, we also have archived tapes covering all our past matches."
"So this is a legitimate operation."
"I'd like to think so."
"And why did Mr. Lebelle assault the man who was on the truck."
"I have no idea. I didn't arrange for him to do it, there were no cameras there. I have not benefited from this scandal."
"But isn't it true you are marketing a new line of WCB action figures with legal themes?"
"What does that have to do with anything?"
"You just said you aren't benefiting from Mr. Lebelle's crime, but according to your production manager, and the receiving departments at no less than twenty-six toy stores I contacted, you have manufactured and started shipping three new action figures with legal themes."
"Well, you're speculating."
"Do you need me to read the press kit?"
"No, that's not really necessary. Is this relevant? I mean, so what if I

made an action figure based on, let's say, you. I was a witness to the actual fight. In fact, I was hit in the leg by the guy when he was trying to come at Mr. Lebelle with the wood. Maybe I'm just reflecting reality. Maybe I have an action figure coming out that comes with a piece of wood."

"Wood?"

"Yes, the accuser on the night in question picked up a piece of wood."

"For what reason?"

"To hit us."

"To hit you?"

"He hit me on the way to trying to hit Mr. Lebelle, but I got in between the two men."

"When did this occur?"

"Well I was standing next to Mr. Lebelle."

"And he hit you both?"

"No, just me. I forced him back against the wall, when I looked to my right Mr. Lebelle was pinned to the wall by the police."

"Was Mr. Jobriath's sweater tucked in?"

"Sweater? He was wearing a wife-beater, from what I recall."

"And where was the hot dog?"

"The hot dog?"

"Before the fighting did Mr. Lebelle hand you anything?"

"I don't remember."

"No hot dog crosses your mind?"

"Crosses my mind, hot dog? No."

Towell sneered, noticing the empty VCR and television in the court. Why were there no cameras that night, the biggest showdown in the history of bowling, and no cameras, no pins, no score machine anywhere in sight.

"And Hulk Hogan, can you explain how he fits into this?"

"I wish I could. How am I supposed to do that? You have to understand, I've been out in that hallway for about four hours, I didn't catch the trailers or the first half of this," Towell said, cutting himself off, stunned. He continued, trying to be calm. "What about Hulk Hogan?"

The Crown stepped it up, cleared his throat and calmly slugged back some of his ice water. The clerk fidgited, waiting for the rest of the story to unravel.

"Mr. Lebelle claims Mr. Jobriath reminded him of Hulk Hogan who one of your bowlers copied for his character?"

"I'm not sure, are you suggesting 'Hollywood' Dragan Momchilo took his name from 'Hollywood' Hulk Hogan?"

"That's what it says in the statement."

"I haven't read the statement lately. Is that the one where Dragan tucks in his sweater, and the guy who Mr. Lebelle punched had a tucked in sweater?"

"Yes."

"I just know the guy attacked us first and I don't remember if Lebelle handed me the hot dog. How Dragan's sweater and Mr. Hogan play into this trial doesn't concern me."

"But these are your employees."

"I have nothing more to offer the courts. I want to leave."

"Sir, you are under oath."

"Dragan Momchilo is 5 foot 11, Hulk Hogan is 6 foot 7, I really don't think Mr. Lebelle confused the two, and Hogan isn't an employee of mine. I know that Mr. Lebelle doesn't like Hulk Hogan, and that when we were on tour we'd often watch Hulk Hogan movies to tease Mr. Lebelle. I didn't know he held this resentment with such precision, and wanted to vent it on the provincial level."

"Did Mr. Lebelle hand you anything before the confrontation with Mr. Jobriath?"

"Mr. Jobriath is what, 5 foot 9? I think it's clear that he does not, nor does anyone in this courtroom resemble Hulk

When I was finally allowed to leave the stand, I just kept walking. I noticed the court clerk was in fact wearing bowling shoes. I knew someone would tell me who won later, I just didn't want to be sitting with the misfits on Team Lebelle anymore. If anyone out there is reading this memoir, someone still owes me a slice of cheesecake and a hot dog. I have no childhood memories of breathing. I replaced these disjointed and unreliable memories with the disjointed and unreliable "Hollywood" Dragan Momchilo, as we photoshopped his unprofessional smile out for violent layouts. Only this time, with WCB, I have brought hostages with me. That night in August was the turning point for WCB. Most people are weapons before they are nests. It sounds melodramatic, but that is the main ingredient of my life. Without it, I'd just be water and income tax. I was glad it was coming to an end. In many ways, insanity is an option, like vegetarianism, or whether or not one recycles. I made a conscious decision to evacuate the lockerroom of the unwell as soon as the opportunity presented itself. I had to escape.

— FROM *THE MAN WHO MURDERED BOWLING*

Hogan. What is important is that we are sitting here, wasting taxpayer's money on a two-punch fight and the guy came at both of us with a piece of wood. I was too busy trying to figure out what I was going to do to remember a hot dog, all right?"

The Crown finished the interview with Towell famously quipping, "Bowling is not responsible for this. It was a two-punch fight. This isn't what I did on my summer vacation versus the province of Ontario with a side of bowling. Don't you people have anything better to do? Is this what God wants us to be doing? I don't think so."

Refusing to stay to hear the verdict, Robert Towell left the building and paged Nikola.

As he exited the courthouse, he jumped up into the air and screamed, "This trial is a pig circus." He felt like some sort of Earthbound astronaut. A big smile crossed his lips, followed by a healthy dose of Queen Street exhaust, the air of freedom.

Within ten minutes of nervous pacing and self-muttering, Nikola Towell pulled up to the same patch of street she had pulled away from earlier in the day and allowed her husband to pour into the passenger's side. "How was it?" Nikola asked.

"This reporter says, a pig circus baby, a fucking pig circus. I left. I am assuming they're assassinating him for bowling as we speak."

"So you didn't stay for the result?"

"That's what the 6 o'clock news is for. It was tiring, let's just get some take-out and have sex all night. Turn off the cell, I don't want any insanity leaking in for the rest of the day."

The next morning, a slew of Internet fanatics had posted their versions of what they thought had happened at the trial, based on rumours and second-hand accounts.

Towell refused to read the faxes that came into his home office.

He had shouting contests with Jerry Tomlin: "I just don't care about this now, it's all a big joke. An explosive cake. He got what, three months house arrest, and took my company down with him? I just need time. You run things, however you want, release something. Produce a musical, set a soccer field on fire. Raise global awareness. Do what you think is right."

BOWLING *Weekly*

June 3, 2000

CLOSING TIME?
The Final Days of World
Championship Bowling

FCC INVESTIGATION
Bowlers mocked and used in new DVD

Unapologetic Towell tells PBA:
"I hate your sport"

Unapologetic Towell tells PBA:
"I hate your sport"

FCC to investigate special features section of new WCB DVD

Tuesday, June 3, 2000

(BBN) The release of WCB's pay-per-views from the years 1997 and 1998 will be the subject of an FCC investigation, following complaints that PBA bowlers "were being mocked and used in video distortion" on the special features section of three new DVDs from the controversial bowling company.

Bowling promoter and former child television star Robert Towell did not apologize Monday to anyone who was offended when his company, World Championship Bowling (WCB), released their new line of pay-per-views on DVD and VHS with blatant use of PBA bowling footage, "cleverly" as one PBA board member put it, disguised by distortion. Cleverly, but not enough, according to Jim Certs of the FCC who has fielded numerous complaints from bowlers' family members, agents coaches and sponsors who are sickened by the desparaging portrayals of their athletes on Towell's show. Robert Towell's flagship pay-per-view, BOWLBRAWL will not take place this March due to the company's decision to retool its production

schedule with so many of its athletes caught up in other pursuits. "This is Towell's idea of marketing: publicity and sensationalism. But by the time we get through with this, his BOWLBRAWL pay-per-views, or whatever they're called won't have a single sponsorship," Certs told BBN.

Many feel Towell deliberately used recognizable bowlers from the PBA due to his resentment of the firm and in part due to their continual denial of his entry onto their board. "The PBA was completely unaware of it. It was not my intention that it go as far as it did. But it did. I'm tired of this sport having no future. I needed to demonstrate the lack of charisma in these athletes. My audience loves my bowlers; they don't care if I make fun of those idiots. So I'm sorry for nothing. I have my sponsors and PBA has theirs. All I want is to demonstrate the context for WCB's brand, which is, to liven up the Latin of sports," Towell said.

Backgammon Ltd. is distributing the DVDs across Canada and have had no complaints from stores or buyers. "It's moving all the time, in some cities we can't keep them in the warehouse, so if there is a problem we're not hearing about it," said Backgammon sales manager Clyde Hudhall.

The DVDs feature a lengthy retrospective collection of all of WCB's previous pay-per-views, plus interviews and bowler profiles of Jordan Binner, Greg Lebelle, Dragan Momchilo, Black Ninja Six and Black Ninja Seven. The PBA "rip-off segments" according to PBA public relations manager Bill Wyatt, is "a blatant misrepresentation of our bowlers."

On Monday, Federal Communications Commission Chairman Michael Powelz ordered an investigation of the incident.

An estimated 14,000 people have seen the trailers, which run at the beginning of the VHS versions and in the special features versions of all new WCB DVDs. The trailers have been taken down from WCB.COM.

Powelz told BBN he was not convinced the use of the PBA players was an accident. "Clearly somebody had knowledge of it. Clearly it was something that was planned by someone," he said. "Towell and his company got what they were looking for."

WCB executive consultant Jerry Tomlin, who is also employed as an on-air personality for WCB, said the incident "was not a malfunction of the archives labeling system and the use of the PBA bowlers was done so sparingly any infringement was not intentional." Tomlin said unauthorized copies of the trailers were appearing on the Internet, before the authorized ones went up at the site, so WCB tried to push the release date of the DVDs and videos up.

WCB.COM posted this tease on its web site last week: "Robert Towell's *BOWLBRAWL* previews promises shocking moments."

Powelz said he was watching the DVD Sunday evening with friends and found the clips to be outrageous and unprofessional.

Beyond using actual PBA footage, Towell hired homeless people to play the parts of has-been bowlers. As they mumbled their lines, talking about the good old days, their names and statistics popped up below them.

"That was the disgusting part of the DVD, the extent to which Towell wants to shock and piss off the *real* bowling community," Certs added.

"I knew immediately it would cause great outrage among the bowling community, which it did," Powelz said, citing "thousands" of complaints received by Monday morning. "We have a very angry bowling public on our hands."

— FROM *BOWLING WEEKLY*

Towell To Give Speech At PBA Final

December 18, 2000

Robert Towell, 28, will present a speech to media and a group of high school students attending the PBA world championships next March in Cleveland, Ohio as part of his community services. The speech will cover the ways in which bowling is used in the media, and will take place as part of the bowling blitz weekend. The speech comes at a strange time in Towell's life, as he is without a bowling company since the demise of WCB (World Championship Bowling). When asked why he was giving a speech, Towell said, "For my crimes against humanity."

Many feel it's a good move on Towell's part, if he ever hopes to get into the PBA's good books. Last year Towell shocked the bowling world with his blatant misrepresentation of PBA players on his now defunct WCB brand of DVDs. "I'm quite honoured to be given this platform and opportunity to give back," said Towell in a phone interview. "I really want to extend my thanks to the PBA for the invitation." There has been no word from Greg Lebelle whose infamous plea at his trial last April ended in the judge ruling against him for what he believed to be "a stupid bowling story" for Lebelle's defense. Towell and Lebelle have not spoken since the trial. Dragan Momchilo, the other mainstay name from WCB has been seen at many local soccer tournaments. A close friend says Momchilo, now 22, has no plans on returning to "that other sport" anytime soon.

—Associate Press

THE LAST OF THE GREATS

March 9, 2001

On the eve of his retirement, Greg Lebelle must be recognized as being the best of his generation and knowing when to leave the sport. But is there a bowler to take his place?

Somewhere between lane fifteen and seventeen a kinship was struck between the sports fan and the legendary macabre theatre of the brute. Somewhere, within those inches of space, Greg Lebelle lost the urge to fight. One explosive night out, letting off steam with WCB owner Robert Towell at a local bar, he wandered into the thinly veiled yarn of myth and reality. He tore through that thread and wound up in Hell. The trial was real, but it wasn't necessary. Think of all the two-punch fights that get separated and forgotten. But there was more on the line than a simple assault charge, it was Lebelle's entire life, assumed violent, assumed thug, because of his size, his muscle, his appearance, and nothing else. As Towell said famously at the trial, "This is not about bowling, this is about what I saw. I saw the accused hit second, throw a punch second, not first. That you think because Lebelle works for my company that I am,

or bowling is, in any way, liable or relevant to this case is embarrassing. I saw what I just explained, plain and simple, you have chosen to create an illusory context, where size and aggression are measured by the pound, where intent is measured by the pound. The fact that this man, who came charging at both Lebelle and I with a piece of wood from his truck, can barely form a sentence in his defense, but is the fan-favourite this afternoon, disgusts me."

It was said that Lebelle's statement alluded to WCB, and that in his drunken state, Greg Lebelle began to assume his character, and believed that the man with whom he was arguing, was in fact his rival,

"Hollywood" Dragan Momchilo.

But as a man to deal with, Lebelle was usually helpful and easy to look up to. He emanated physical courage. He was a street fighting man who had learned how to deal with intimidation during his tough early days on the east coast and out west as a teenager. This was why Momchilo failed to "spook" him. "His own story," says Black Ninja Six, who worked with Lebelle, "wasn't made up. He was living and telling his story, twenty-four hours a day. That is what he had to give. He wasn't an athlete, but he was stronger than all of us combined."

After conquering his demons for nearly eleven years, 1999 saw Lebelle change gears and return to the mean streets of his origin, peddling drugs legally, as a harm reduction consultant for street health in Toronto. This, combined with the stress of continued live appearances, controlled fighting, and living as what he called "an artificial cog" rather than as a part of "something connected to the human concern," propelled Lebelle to leave WCB and his bowling dynasty behind.

"Things were already over by the time the trial drew near," says Towell, who took the stand as key witness to the assault. "It was a strain. Of the six testimonies, five were character witnesses, mine was about the event itself."

Towell says there was time to prepare, "I didn't have a lawyer, I didn't need one, the case didn't really involve me, but I think that is how Lebelle wanted it, a way to create a wedge between myself, bowling and himself. It was the ultimate tribute, I think, a strange way of saying goodbye. Only he and I know the truth. There are sometimes no words, do you understand?"

Currently, Lebelle continues to serve the community in the harm reduction field. "I'm a genuine fighter, because I know what it is to lose," Lebelle says, taking a long harsh drag of his cigarette as one of his clients approaches. "I have a job to do now, these are my people."

With a rumoured $24,000 on the table for a rematch with Momchilo – the opponent whose face he once promised to render unrecognizable to his beloved grandmother – Lebelle pushed the stack of cash away.

This Saturday, on one of his only days off in weeks, he will be at home when Robert Towell delivers his speech at the PBA tournament, perhaps the last we'll ever see of anyone from the famed WCB legacy. "I think it's fitting," Lebelle surmises. "He started it, and it will be great to see if he can carry on in mainstream bowling, not that he ever needed them, but I'll be watching from the comfort of my couch, rather than locking up with photographers and hot dog vendors."

When asked about his long

time rival, Momchilo, Lebelle shrugged, "I thought he was okay, I thought he was confused about a lot of things. There was something odd about the guy, he was missing something, something that other people have on a basic level that make them consistent."

Lebelle says he enjoyed his time with WCB but in the end was convinced that it was not where he wanted to end up. "I just thought that I could help people. WCB is entertainment, it's fantasy, it isn't the streets. I was just a puppet, even though I was being creative, and well-received, I knew deep down that I was just an adopted asshole, I knew that I had to be a part of something more humbling."

Momchilo fought with his heart, Godfrey fought with enthusiasm, but Lebelle fought and moved in the business with his brain. While he beat everyone into a shadow, one of the greatest memories sports fans have of Lebelle is him taking on the local league champions during WCB's first season. He'd rip their plaid shirts in two, get two strikes in a row, throw them into the next lane. None it seemed had the power to knock him out.

After his humiliation at the cleats of Momchilo's soccer squad, Lebelle fought more conservatively in his rematches with Momchilo, living in fear of the sucker punch, and would take a bland win on point-spread rather than get into a high-risk slugfest.

Towell called him "the incredible bulk."

With this vast bulk, his thick shoulders and his pawing slap, Lebelle brought order to the WCB locker room. "I never saw him in a gym, but I did see him on his bike one time. He looked like a rhino, he could do it all; he seemed to reach out to all of us for awhile, and really made his presence felt."

Whether it was a house show, pay-per-view or toy store appearance, Greg Lebelle was always consistent, always genuine, and always there to do the job. "I never wanted him to stray from who he really was, I always knew the real Greg Lebelle. He was able, because of his superior intellect, to just play a character. I think the trial and the end of WCB was good for him," Towell confided.

Momchilo has not seen the former WCB champion since their infamous cage match at WCB DEVASTATION, though he did speak to him on the phone before the trial. "He wished me luck, and I believe he was being genuine," says Lebelle.

— FROM *BOWLING WEEKLY*

WCB OPERATION BOWLFILL

PBA Finals
Cleveland, Ohio
March 10, 2001

Scratch: Without benefit of handicap; actual score.

Semi-fingertip: A ball drilling that allows the ball to rest on the pads between the second and third joints of the third and fourth fingers. More powerful than a conventional grip, less powerful than a full fingertip grip, it is generally not recommended.

Semi-roller: A ball that rolls on a track just outside the thumb-hole. Also called a semi-spinner. This type of ball is considered the most powerful and has displaced the full-roller in professional bowling.

Robert Towell and Jerry Tomlin snickered to one another as the PBA's brass walked past their open dressing room door. "Do you hear that?" Jerry said. "It's nuts out there." He cut a piece of club sandwich off a plate with a knife, and offered it to Robert.

"No thanks," Robert said.

At exactly 2:15 PM, Robert Towell could hear an announcement regarding his upcoming speech. "They were so organized and there were about seventeen camera operators, and personnel everywhere. Assistants and grips, grip's assistants, club sandwich repairmen, catering squads, medicine men and women, helicopter blade washers, merchants, vendors, and those suspected of being vendors all clamoured around the mid-sized arena in the heart of Cleveland, Ohio. I just remember the number of fat men in the building. Obese men, some darned in stubble, some clever enough to succumb to proper grooming conditions for the new millennium – including nasal hair evacuation, armpit hair trimming and proper eyebrow density – scurried and strutted in their blue ESPN blazers."

Robert Towell, dressed in a borrowed ESPN crested blazer, sported a T-shirt with Lebelle's headshot. Around his neck he wore aviator glasses. He took his pirate patch from its casing and put it over his right eye. Then he put a pair of aviator glasses over both eyes.

A floor director entered the dressing room. "Are you almost ready? They said anytime." One of his assistants poured Towell a glass of water, the other handed him a lemon wedge. They were trained, "like dolphin clock-parts," Towell later recalled.

Jerry nodded to the floor director, "Yes, everything is ready."

Towell backed him up. "Redemption." He delivered a scowl into the mirror and began to speak in a bad actor's voice: "Oh dear PBA how I was so wrong to mock you on DVD, let me make it up to you by doing this public service announcement, like the ten commandments only with a proper jingle."

"Sounds good boss."

"Let's do this."

"You need your speech?" Jerry asked.

Robert Towell wasn't listening. "I coulda been one of the boys," he said, flexing his muscles under his blazer.

Jerry Tomlin brought over the plate of food. "It's going to be fine," he said.

The floor director resurfaced and pulled his head in a backwards motion, signalling that speed and immediate physical reaction were required. As he later wrote in his memoir: "As I started walking out with Tomlin by my side, I could feel the energy of the audience, and I saw a lot of people I knew in the crowd, which actually worked against me, because I find it's hard to lie in a mixed crowd. I much prefer playing to the unconverted."

"Okay sir, anytime you're ready to address the crowd."

"Right," Towell said, nibbling on a french fry from his plate. "I can't believe they let us in the building," Towell said to Tomlin, who was finishing his part of the notorious Cleveland club sandwich.

"Oh Rob, don't worry, that's all behind us," Jerry Tomlin said.

"Not that far behind us. Here, keep close to me," Towell said, throwing Jerry a pickle from his plate. "And make sure your walkie-talkie thing is on," Robert said with a wink.

"Ladies and gentlemen, now to give a speech entitled *The Slow Revolution from Lane Sixteen*, president and owner of World Championship Bowling, will you please give a warm Ohio welcome to Robert Towell."

Walking towards the crowd he felt something deep within, a knotted wave. He grabbed the press conference microphone from its stand in one hand and with the other threw the full pitcher of ice water onto the ESPN registration table directly below him, ruining a perfectly good club sandwich in the process. "Sorry about that," he cackled. The bacon became a wet rubbery tongue no one would stick inside their mouth. Not tonight anyway, tonight was going to be magic.

The cameraman, father of two, and a former professional bowler, had just finished his sandwich and had remarked to the catering girl, only moments earlier, how much he had enjoyed it, that it was one of the best he had ever consumed. These things would unravel; Towell let them, he had time to kill. Things were happening above ground, things were being attached to vents, sixteen vents to be exact.

Robert Towell adjusted the corporate PBA logo microphone and winked at the camera operator.

"Hello everyone. Before I start, I would like to acknowledge my gratitude to both ESPN and the PBA for allowing me this platform. My father taught me many things. He took me to my first pro game when I was only five. When I won, he bought me my own bowling alley. Then, when I turned twenty-four, I started World Championship Bowling." He winked at the caterers he was so enthused. He loved to lie, he dug deeper. "I then burned down the bowling alley my father bought me as a cleansing ritual."

Now, in front of the cameras, some of which were his own, Robert Towell felt no pressure; quite simply he saw a fin cutting through the world in front of him. "I was asked to speak here today about small-scale sports leagues creating a niche for themselves amongst much larger corporate contingencies, wherein a smaller market is created based on a sort of meagre emulation of a very established and satiated nuance of an existing audience, following the rules of the standard governing television protocol. Well, I'm not going to do that. In fact, I'm not going to teach you anything. Instead, I will become the alternative, and in the end, the establishment; and all you bald fatso lowlifes who beat their wives and think TV dinners are some sort of culinary break-through, all you beer-bellied-bastards will be shipped to the sporting has-been hall of fame where you belong. On this great day my wife has launched another line of scarves and boots, as well as a line of fragrances for pet owners, single mothers, unwed mothers, lonely bachelors, even perhaps you bowling tragedies out there watching today, you too could benefit from my wife's new cosmetic efforts. But back to the here and now, the bald and the fat. I see before me today a dirty gross bastard island for loser nobodies. How's that for a doormat? Your masculinity is so far off that we have strict orders from God, who has told me to cast you out, and to rebuild this sport in whatever likeness I choose." He adjusted the microphone in his hand and gazed out slowly across the audience. "You see, you can't change the ending. PBA suits, don't even try going to commercial. You can't change live television. You should have pre-taped this, to secure that old Jimmy Campbell, the hometown favourite would once again win, and make all your pithy sponsors salivate. Well, that's not going to happen. Jimmy Campbell is not even in the building. I have looked over the PBA's list of top bowlers and I am not satisfied. And if I decide to put those PBA losers on television, you'll be the last to know. I'm about to inject a lethal dose of poison into North America's sleeper sport, for the very last time. Lebelle and Momchilo, these men are on their way to your tournament and convention booths, to kiss your wives, destroy your husbands...." Robert began to do a series of gestures, very closely resembling a jig. "You better watch out you better not try, you better untie your shoes I'm telling you why, Momchilo and Lebelle are coming to town."

"Cut his mic, cut the camera, cut to commercial!" one of the floor directors said.

"They'll be here at the top of the hour. These are the men who took my brand, World Championship Bowling, and in three short years did more to destroy it than any other faction. I switched sponsors like underwear. I had to fight their battles with executives, with distributors, toy manufactures, but tonight, they fight for me. And they fight your heroes. The poison has arrived."

A man with red hair in an electric blue ESPN blazer ran to his cameraman, motioning to roll film. Tongue-tied with a mouthful of orange Jell-O, he stammered as Towell's giant hand shadowed a frantic swarm of camera lights. The man with red hair waved hysterically: "Get over here Dan!" Dan wore a red T-shirt and black jeans with an apricot bandanna and ran like a schoolgirl with marbles in her sneakers. He nearly dropped the camera, having to stop abruptly as a caterer carrying a large glazed ham on a platter crossed his path. He dropped a coil of black cable feed and hooked it to the VTR pack, passing a table of club sandwiches being removed one at a time by ESPN employees. Dan's stomach rumbled while passing the pickles, which got their own table. Towell threw a clump of mashed potatoes at the redhead.

"Holly shit, Dan just shoot something else, shoot the scoreboard, or the merchandising booth, anything but the WCB logos!" the redhead barked, scooping the carb mess from his scalp.

In the crowd a group of men gnawed on cooked meat from a sack and passed a small thermos of gravy. "Sam, over here, I need some more."

"Hold on, something weird is going on," Sam Sheldon said, applying black smear under his eyes.

Robert Towell laughed into his microphone. "Look, you can whine all you want, scour the building for WCB minions all you want, we have back-up generators and live web feed, you won't be able to alter this broadcast. This is a foolproof blueprint step-by-step WCB invasion, a finish to the PBA finals that will change history forever. Whatever your cameras shoot goes into our truck. Whatever we shoot, goes live."

Robert Towell talked into his cellphone. "Start to run the WCB/PBA montages, and then prepare the boys for their cameo." Robert Towell returned to his public duty. "Now, as you will notice, WCB logos are being lowered along side your lovely ESPN and PBA logos. Congratulations. You have now evolved, somewhat. And while this may mean great ratings temporarily for the PBA, we are in the midst of sports broadcasting history. History will be made here today in Cleveland."

The crowd began to unravel; some hit the concession stands, some became as pallid as paneled wood, some began gnawing at product with appetites like Greg Lebelle's at a late seventies salad bar.

Springing from behind a curtain emerged a rejuvenated Jordan Binner who tossed some boxes of WCB merchandise into the vendor booths, including WCB INVASION T-shirts, taking some unsuspecting sales reps out in the process. Then he wheeled in Dale Godfrey, who was unable to walk.

A frantic ESPN personality began an impromptu interpretation of the hysteria. "Hello, I have been informed all doors have been locked and are not being opened until the show goes off the air. ESPN coverage will continue until we have word from our producer. In case you are just tuning in, this is a historical moment in the PBA circuit. ESPN has been covering this event for years, and I've been privileged to be a part of many years of coverage as a fan and basic cable or pay-per-view subscriber. But never did we ever fathom this guerrilla media attack by a rival bowling company would take place on live television. Here I stand in front of my fellow journalists and reporters, representing the sporting press, and here I watch the end of a great tradition. This is Paul Taylor of ESPN apologizing. Whether you will even hear this broadcast I don't know. We were all here attending a scheduled pre-match lecture by Robert Towell, the famed indie bowling mogul, and what was set to be a casual talk has turned into an impromptu bowling hostage crisis. WCB officials assure us no harm will be done to anyone, that they will be set free after the event is over."

Robert Towell signalled his orange clad cotton lackeys to turn one of the catering tables into a WCB news desk. The backs of their golf shirts read SECURITY, a giant farce that tickled Robert in his laugh lines.

"Boss we need you back here, they have to talk to you about the trucks."

"Yeah, sure no problem. Get Godfrey and Binner on play-by-play immediately."

As WCB officials scurried throughout the building, chirping into microphones, Towell calmly brushed his chest, as if fixing his proud feathers. His Lebelle T-shirt was crisp, and hundreds were on hand at concession stands. Some of the more aggressive interns took over beer tents and popcorn stands to make room for additional WCB merchandise. "That's right, just like we did at the food court, during the merchant war drill, that great practice run which has so obviously made you who you are today, my most valuable assets, my loyal WCB employees. You'll get good reference letters, you'll do your parents proud," Towell laughed watching the ESPN announcers try to explain to their home viewers the WCB wash. Paul Taylor and Jim Preswick stood dumfounded, jaws anchored stiff. The mood turned crab red.

"Ladies and gentlemen, I thank you for staying with us in this uncertain technical situation in our broadcast," Jim Preswick said firmly.

"That's right Jim," Paul Taylor said supportively. "It's a sensitive situation here at the PBA finals. We are not in danger, yet the new powers that be are keeping us here until the match is over. They are said to be finishing this broadcast, ESPN coverage or not, and it will finish as planned which is at, let me see... Hold on, I'm getting a message from the director. Take over, I'm needed backstage," Paul Taylor said and handed the broadcast over to Jim.

As the announcer unhooked himself from headphone and mic clips, Dale Godfrey clothes-lined him with a short severe stroke. "Nice Dale, right in the throat," cheered his counterpart Jordan Binner. "That's going to look awesome on the replay."

"He totally didn't see that one coming," Godfrey said, and for one minute, the pain in his back, the thousands of children he had sired and the calloused hands that twice daily thumbed the *Toronto Sun* seemed at peace.

Back at ESPN's desk, where some fans had taken up residence and tried to talk to their loved ones at home, the messages were clear, *We aren't in danger, but we're trapped, we don't know for how long.*

"From what we can gather, it looks as though Robert Towell and his superstars Momchilo and Lebelle are all here in Cleveland and ready to wage war against those bowlers in the PBA."

From the ESPN bunker Paul Taylor, with an ice pack across his throat, took his camera operator in front of the makeshift WCB desk, where Jordan Binner helped Godfrey wedge his wheelchair under the table.

Jordan patched through to Towell's intercom: "Yeah Rob, we're ready in five."

Jerry Tomlin sat backstage with Momchilo. Slowly Tomlin hand-fed ice to Momchilo who was deep in the midst of a nightmare. A nightmare to which no action figure series could do justice.

"He's suppose to be outside terrorizing the crowd, heckling the PBA merchants!" Towell yelled from the hallway.

"No, he can't move, he's freaking out, just pouring with sweat," Tomlin assured Towell.

"I don't care, this is it, this is the big swerve, the finale, the end of the season, like on Dallas when Pam walks into the shower and sees Bobby instead of Grayson. This is it, the biggest moment in televised sport."

Momchilo absorbed the poetry of all he had conquered. His father's respect, the respect of the business of sports, the camaraderie, vilification and redemption, of his sweater's whereabouts at his waistline; he wanted nothing more than to come clean, he couldn't lie; he wanted something to leave behind, a new face, a new body, a different side. His best friend, business partner, and mismatched male counterpart had been swallowed by a simple game. No amount of revenge tonight would alter the course of his consciousness. He would have to walk away, he would have to be strong.

"What's wrong?"

"Oh nothing Rob, just that, from what you've told me Greg beat some guy up and was arrested because he thought the guy was me."

"I keep telling you that is just what he told the court. Greg knew he was going to lose, he had like 26 priors. There was no way they would have believed him no matter what he said, at least he was thinking of you. Now get out there with Lebelle and show them who the fuck runs the show. Us. Not these lame corporate sponsored lowbrow idiots."

Momchilo noticed Jerry Tomlin on his cell phone, and pushed past Towell. "Jerry is that Dale? Give me your phone."

"Sure, here," Jerry Tomlin said, handing over the phone.

"Dale, fuck can't we leave, can't we go in your truck for a bit? I just need to clear my head. My grandmother is watching at home, how can I explain this life? My father was an international soccer star, and, please Dale, I can't go out there."

"I don't know what to tell you buddy, I think we're locked in here, I don't know, I think we'll have to wait and go through with it."

"I just have to leave," Momchilo said. He tossed the phone.

"Here, drink this ice water," Tomlin said.

As the ice melted and the water churned Momchilo thought hard about the world around him, and his fallen comrade, delusional on the stand, blaming a sport for his rage. Dragan Momchilo stood up, spitting the remaining ice from his mouth as Lebelle entered the hallway from the washroom, knowing the man, the beast friend who joked that he was raised by yaks, wanted nothing more than to crawl off the back of this world, like a flimsy barcode, and explode into a constellation. He wanted to be as old as lye, and removable with a fingernail. But there would be one last run, and this was it.

Greg Lebelle, recently smuggled over the border, thick and doused with patchouli, entered the room like a cloud. Momchilo knew the man well, a person to slalom through with ideas before retiring to bed, to clear his head of alien rape nightmares, a crazed plush animal at a fair.

"I remember the day Greg phoned me up and told us the news," Robert Towell said, hand tightening up his belt in the men's room. The ESPN crew were sulking in the stalls, but filming their captor all the same. "This will be good for the lawsuit," one of them boasted. But Towell was confident that day; he washed his hands as he spoke, careful not to leave any remaining bright pink foam on his hands. Towell, ever the opportunist, continued his lecture. "Now I know you think I'm some sort of circus ring leader, but these are real people, those who work for me. Now, let me explain to you something about Greg Lebelle, the one you seem set to vilify. He phoned me up and told us the news. Not only would it mean no main eventing for four months, it meant something more: the testicle would have to come out."

The men in the stalls came out of the toilets and began washing their hands. Their faces said, *Tell us the rest of the story;* though they made no effort to speak directly, their expensive equipment assured Towell he was at least going to be on the news at some point.

"The three of us went for a walk, it was around Christmas time, and Greg started to tell us the story," Towell said, pushing down on the paper towel dispenser. "So anyway, he took us for this walk and told us what had happened to him when he was sixteen."

Greg Lebelle entered both the shot and the washroom and continued where Towell had just left off. "When I was sixteen," Lebelle started, "in prison in Edmonton, they had me in the lock up and they spread my legs apart, kicked me so hard in the balls they ripped the sack, these fucking military cops."

As he continued, the hairs on the scrotums in the room began to tingle, not out of recognition or sympathy, but gratitude. His testicle lay in a Styrofoam cup of ice in the Emergency foyer of the prison. He would later be transferred to a proper hospital.

For a moment, before the bathroom cleared, Greg imagined the simple seamless afternoons with Richard, his twin brother, carefree sunstroke moments, coming out of the Atlantic Ocean, New Brunswick's cold salty world. And how they used to catch eels by simply swimming deep into the weeds and playing dead, then return wrapped in the slimy fortune. All afternoon, no fishing license, no parental influence or Kodak nostalgia. Twenty years later. The cancer latched on to the instable tissue, attaching itself with the subtlety of a kite tail.

Robert Towell returned to the podium. "Hello. Is this still working? Boys in the van you hear me? Good. In case you people didn't know, I am Robert Towell, and you aren't going anywhere. As you can see, my men are taking care of your so called athletes, yeah, go on, film over there," Robert pointed to the small stage where the PBA had planned on awarding the championship.

"I have back-up cameras with a feed to my own personal satellite; I have my own VTR guy in a van waiting in case these ESPN assholes decide to shut down their coverage. Just keep shooting boys, everyone. The doors have been locked. Sit down and enjoy the show. My boys are going to weed through your loser heroes, and by the end of this boring annual ritual of gluttony, one of the monsters, one of my vials of poison will walk out of here the undisputed PBA tour champion. I hope I'm not giving away too much here. Now we're going live to my colour commentary team covering this event at centre-lane, Jordan Binner and Dale Godfrey. Boys, how is it going down there?"

Dale Godfrey sat in a wheelchair wearing a jean jacket with no shirt underneath. His toque had a small crown on it, and there were small-framed photos of his various children on his side of the desk. His tanned muscles from time to time offered a glimpse at his sporting past, but too often a pain shot through his lower back and caused him to wince. He shrugged it off with a smile, nodding to his broadcast partner Jordan Binner. Binner watched as a lanky bird-faced twenty-year old choked on her popcorn. "She shouldn't be here, she should be at home knitting and teaching her younger brother long division. This is the PBA, right Dale?"

"Yes it is, my son," Godfrey said with a smirk.

"I mean come on, were you folks at home really going to sit through three hours of comb-overs and those two idiots over there doing play-by-play?" Jordan and Dale waved to the ESPN control desk. The men waved back.

"Rob, we're live at lane sixteen where one of our first three qualifying matches is going to take place, featuring one of the WCB superstars. We believe it's Momchilo, Dragan Momchilo, the Serbian god of bowling. A former European champion and six-time Ajax bowler of the month. He should be arriving anytime now to face Frank Billington, of Akron, Ohio. Frank is a former State champion, and ranks 36th among bowlers nationally in championship tournaments. As for Momchilo, he is as yet unranked in PBA competition, but I hear we have some footage of him training?"

"That's right Dale, and we'll get to it soon. I hear that Dragan has been training hard for this tournament. Not only does he want to help our brand of World Championship Bowling survive, but he wants his grandmother to see him victorious tonight, and we certainly hope he doesn't disappoint her."

"No. Can't let Grandma down."

"No. Certainly not. To disappoint ones grandmother, on such an auspicious evening as the PBA championship would be detrimental. Let's hope he qualifies in this, the first of three matches he'll have to win to advance to the championship final."

"Folks, for those just tuning in, we've covered many WCB events over the years before being shut down, but this is something special. I'd like to thank our WCB security who have sealed the building so you folks in the audience won't leave, and you'll get to witness bowling history in the making! For those at home, remember to login to WCB.COM if you have any trouble watching this telecast with your existing cable hook-up. And you can also order your own World Championship Bowling T-shirt; not only is it black, its black and red."

"And it says something on the back doesn't it?"

"It sure does Jordan. It says, *Mission Accomplished*. Not bad, eh?"

"Now we're going to take a look at a special video montage to give the folks at home a bit of history on WCB."

"I hope I'm in this one," Godfrey said, rubbing his hands together.

The ESPN crew members shook their heads, hapless at the controls. They watched the grainy footage fill all the screens. "It looks like it was shot on security cameras," one of them said.

"I heard some of it was."

"What are we suppose to tell our sponsors?"

"Forget the sponsors, what are we gonna tell the PBA, their whole show is being hijacked right now."

"We should try to override their broadcast, cause a black out of the channels or something."

"But he's taping this and broadcasting it on the web; this isn't one hook up, he's figured out a way to keep things running even if we shut down."

Back in the bowling alley Binner and Godfrey watched the montage come to an end. Robert Towell fed them lines. "Okay, Jordan talk about the history of the PBA title and how it's going to be handed over to WCB. For the first time, their champion will surrender."

The recreational bowling extremist group, who had been sending Robert Towell threatening letters leading up to his arrival in Cleveland, snuck by security. They scurried around for positions in the crowd. They convened every fifteen minutes in the men's room. The youngest was lanky Rotten Pop Joe and he carried most of the equipment.

"I can't get a clean shot, not from here, we gotta, fuck, we gotta get a clean shot. This is like we've gone back in time to save the world, I can almost see our names in the papers."

"Ah quit your fantasizing Hank, and check your barrels. Don't want any screw-ups."

The extremist group, lead by Sam Sheldon, unfolded a map of the building.

"I told you to hold it still," Sam Sheldon said, nodding at Rotten Pop Joe, who shook nervously with the map. Hank began to load his gun quietly. He screwed the silencer on top of the tip. "Now boys, let's convene in the men's room at oh-nine-hundred hours. The duffel bags are stowed away in the ceiling. Got it? The tear gas is in them bags, then we run, kidnap Towell, kill him, save the world, you know."

"Yes boss," Rotten Pop Joe said, sipping on a can of cola; his balloon lips were a garden of cankers and cold sores.

Robert Towell continued badgering the audience, waging a war of belly moans and grammatically incorrect insults. The delicious news came to his earpiece.

"The trucks are in position, any time you're ready sir," his assistant said calmly.

"Film the crowd for a minute, I want to see the mood," Towell nodded.

Two WCB lackeys unfastened some rope and a giant banner dropped. *WCB: Mission Accomplished.* Lebelle's face was tattooed behind the slogan. For a moment everyone watched the sign drop and cover the PBA logo. Some journalists snapped photographs, as did some fans. From the washroom three bowling hunters emerged well-equipped and ready to chase game. Their first targets were Jordan Binner and Dale Godfrey but a panic washed over the southeast side of the crowd.

"What is that!?" a paying patron cried.

"I think it's sand!" said his friend.

"Where's it coming from?"

"The vent!"

"Holy shit," Godfrey cried, moving his wheelchair out from beneath the broadcast desk, clenching the rubber in his hands, motioning Binner to his side.

"How will we breathe?" said one of the vendors.

Binner unhooked his headset. "I'm trying, the people are all over the place, I think I'm hooked in here, the wires are around my chair."

Rotten Pop Joe secured a safe targeting position beside some tables and chairs.

"Quick, up here Hank," said Sam Sheldon. "Pass me that scope, quick."

Rotten Pop Joe took out a single round and loaded his handgun.

"I told you those small guns were no good, we need accuracy, get the job done. Those are close range guns; we're back here in the cheap killer seats."

The sand poured down around the ankles of Rotten Pop and his friends, the heavy grains pinned them at the ankles, causing them to fall over onto their rifle tripods.

"Fuck, we didn't plan on this, what is going on?" Through the vents the intensity of the sand bent the metal slits. Robert Towell's assistant ran beside him down the hallway. "Sir, the sixth and seventh trucks are in position," she said.

"Fine, tell them to drop their contents now, and signal for the talent to run to the end of lane sixteen, the van's in the back there."

"Back there, quick, hurry," Lebelle said tugging Momchilo. "But first we're suppose to grab that PBA championship trophy and break it."

"This is nuts," Dragan Momchilo said, watching the rivers of sand fill the gutters of the surrounding lanes.

"He must be filming, that's the only explanation; he must be going live, this place is full of cameras," Lebelle began to laugh.

"We work for Satan," Momchilo shouted, bits of sand in his mouth.

"No, he's not that bad. This is fun, better than your wuzzie soccer pantomime," Lebelle snorted.

"Whatever Lebelle, at least it's a real sport."

"What do you call this?"

"Well, let's see, it's psychologically..."

"Yes..."

"... unnecessary."

"Psychologically unnecessary? That's great Dragan, you're really coming into manhood well."

By this time, consumed by the misfortune of having their broadcast desk directly under an open-mouthed vent, Godfrey and Binner were up to their waists in sand. Some of the crew and hunters were toppled when a series of vending machines were pushed over in a panic.

Laughing particularly at the hunters, Robert Towell, complete with megaphone, emerged from the backstage area, now dressed in a white suit that seemed to glow in its simple cotton hue. "Okay boys, meet us at the end of lane sixteen, now. I don't care how you get there, just do it now," Towell instructed with a megaphone. "That went well didn't it?"

"Yes sir, I liked it when you were going on about replacing all their corporate sponsors, then in a fit of dramatic physical irony, just replaced their space with sand."

"Yeah, it was quick."

"What was quick sir?"

"The sand. Get it?"

"Yes sir, that's hilarious."

Outside Lebelle and Momchilo walked towards the van.

"Rob said to wait for five minutes," the stagehand said.

"Five minutes? This place will be Egyptian in five minutes." This was not a normal chain of events, sand on the waxed flooring, the surface being scratched like a pupil, irreversible damage. "Shit, here he comes."

"Okay boys. In the back, let's go." Towell jumped in the driver's seat.

"Dragan, close the door." Momchilo did as Towell instructed. The van leaked quietly out of the parking lot as the first grains of sand penetrated the back of the lanes, knocking down the pins in the process.

"What now?" Lebelle said, looking at the road ahead. Towell drove into the tropical Ohio sky. The highway enveloped them, the grey hugged them, and the cement soothed all of them, swallowed up by the rumble of the late afternoon.

The sky hung heavy, it was bruised, but from what? Towell drove down the stretch of road that resembled everything else that day, long and bright, silent. No one was speaking, everyone's heartbeats and breathing were in sync one last time and one by one Robert Towell dropped them off: Momchilo at a soccer field that seemed to open itself in Adidas crops and shin guard summits, and then the assistants, both of them at the bus station with pithy envelopes full of hundred dollar bills, and finally, perhaps to graze with a like-minded yak of his origin, Lebelle, the giant bowling beast was released into nature.

Lebelle was the last one to leave the car. He took his envelope and nodded.

"Don't call me," said Towell.

"I'm sure I'll find what I'm...."

"And don't hand anyone a hot dog. Yellow police tape isn't a common condiment item, despite what new precedents you've set."

"Okay boss."

"I like to think that you are out there, grazing.

"Oh, I'll be grazing all right."

A few miles ahead Towell saw his wife on the side of the road in her knickers and began to grin. He pulled over and got out.

"Thanks for the ride sailor," Nikola said, handing Rob her suitcase and a bag full of potatoes. With three suitcases full of clothing and memorabilia from an unmatched corporate romance, the Towells smiled into the sunset, and their unleaded fuel leaked out the tailpipe like a sweet kite tail with ribbons.

Robert Towell put on a fresh pair of black lycra driving gloves, pulled his aviator glasses over his eyes, rolled down his window and rubbed Nikola's smooth legs.

"So, somewhere in those bags you packed our passports and cash, and you have the ticket reservations right?"

"Of course Rob," Nikola smiled.

At the same time the Towells noticed the big hot air balloon rising in the sky to the left of them, and both felt calmed by its ascent.

As the night unravelled, the sun began to tuck itself into the highway.

"Did you water the plants?"

"No, I sold them."

"Good."

They were tunneling now, tunneling out of the only burrow they had known. The airport was close, the highway was getting smaller, slowly setting into the skull of the evening sun, as if the slightest gash had been opened up just to let them in.

This was their portal.

Nikola was all smiles and relief, and she wriggled and smiled, preparing for the hours of much needed sloth. Robert too was in a good mood, his former life, like a phantom limb, was barely detectable. Still, there would be side effects to the procedure.

"Do they bowl in Morocco?"

THANKS TO: Janine Armin, Hilary Ash, Warren Auld, Jordan Binner, Black Ninja Six (not Seven), Andy Brown, Michael Bryson, Maihyet Burton, Simon Chan, Katherine Cockshutt, Sarah Cullen, Ian Ferrier, Jon Paul Fiorentino, Dale Godfrey, Bret Hart, Michael Holmes, Alison Honey, Ibi Kaslik, Andy Kaufman, Catherine Kidd, rob mclennan, Lesley Metcalfe, Lori McNamara, Hal Niedzviecki, Scott Nihill, Thomas C. Norden, Alexis O'Hara, Geoffrey Pugen, Marty Spellerberg, Martina Sorbara, Victoria Stanton, Dagmara Stephan, Jerry Tomlin, Nikola Towell, RM Vaughan, Paul Vermeersch, Erin Vollick, Al Zabas.

SPECIAL THANKS TO: Robert Towell for allowing me to excerpt from *The Man Who Murdered Bowling*. As of this writing it remains unpublished.

	7 −	⑦ /	9 ⁄	5 4	9 ⁄	F ⁄	☒	8 ⁄	☒	☒☒ 9
.	7	15	30	39	49	69	89	109	139	168	168

TEAM BOWLBRAWL:

Young Robert Towell drawing, Bowlbrawl logo, WCB logo and other interior designs by Marty Spellerberg.

Back cover photography by Simon Chan.

Other photos by Simon Chan, Alison Honey, and Katherine Cockshutt.

Promo videos by Geoffrey Pugen.

Fashion photos and drawing by Maihyet Burton / Lilith Clothing.

NATHANIEL G. MOORE is an iconoclast, fighter and lover. *BOWLBRAWL* is his first book.